THRIVING AS A MINORITY-OWNED BUSINESS IN CORPORATE AMERICA

BUILDING A PATHWAY TO SUCCESS FOR MINORITY ENTREPRENEURS

William Michael Cunningham

Apress®

Thriving As a Minority-Owned Business in Corporate America: Building a Pathway to Success for Minority Entrepreneurs

William Michael Cunningham
WASHINGTON, DC, United States

ISBN-13 (pbk): 978-1-4842-7239-8   ISBN-13 (electronic): 978-1-4842-7240-4
https://doi.org/10.1007/978-1-4842-7240-4

Managing Director, Apress Media LLC: Welmoed Spahr
Acquisitions Editor: Shivangi Ramachandran
Development Editor: Matthew Moodie
Coordinating Editor: Rita Fernando

Cover designed by eStudioCalamar

Distributed to the book trade worldwide by Springer Science+Business Media New York, 233 Spring Street, 6th Floor, New York, NY 10013. Phone 1-800-SPRINGER, fax (201) 348-4505, e-mail orders-ny@springer-sbm.com, or visit www.springeronline.com. Apress Media, LLC is a California LLC and the sole member (owner) is Springer Science + Business Media Finance Inc (SSBM Finance Inc). SSBM Finance Inc is a **Delaware** corporation.

For information on translations, please e-mail booktranslations@springernature.com; for reprint, paperback, or audio rights, please e-mail bookpermissions@springernature.com.

Apress titles may be purchased in bulk for academic, corporate, or promotional use. eBook versions and licenses are also available for most titles. For more information, reference our Print and eBook Bulk Sales web page at http://www.apress.com/bulk-sales.

Supplementary material referenced by the author in this book is available to readers on GitHub (https://github.com/Apress/thriving-minority-owned-business).

Printed on acid-free paper

Dedicated to:

*My father, Paul Nicholas Cunningham Sr.,
my big brother, Paul Nicholas Cunningham Jr.,
my sister, Pamela Lynn Cunningham*

My beloved Aunts

Catherine Harrison

Geraldine Harrison Bland

Bertha Harrison Saunders

Marrietta Harrison Arrington Whitaker

Henrietta Harrison Jerman

Joyce Harrison Park, DDS

Rosa Harrison Lee Kyler

and, of course, my mother

Marie Harrison Cunningham

Written for

*Aunt Ruth Nelson (95 and still going strong...)
...and, for the youngest, Anaya.*

Contents

About the Author

William Michael Cunningham is an economist, investment advisor, researcher, and social investing policy analyst. Cunningham researches, evaluates, develops, and creates specific socially responsible investments.

He is founder of Creative Investment Research, MinorityBank.com, DiversityFund.net, and MinorityFinance.com. Mr. Cunningham is the author of *The JOBS Act: Crowdfunding for Small Businesses and Startups*, published by Apress. He spoke at Northwestern University's Kellogg School of Management, at the Harvard Business School, and at the Wharton School of Business DC Innovation Summit. He has given talks on impact investing in Finland, Switzerland, England, and Germany.

As a strong advocate for the integration of human values in finance, he develops new ways to combine social values and investing. His work includes creating some of the first ESG impact measurement methodologies and work on blockchain and cryptocurrency. Mr. Cunningham has been responsible for many innovative impact investing approaches, including the following: Maternal Mortality Reparation Facility for Black Women. https://www.prlog.org/12876083-maternal-mortality-reparation-facility-for-black-women.html; Green Mortgage Backed Security - https://www.creativeinvest.com/EnergyEfficientMortgageMBSJune2006.pdf; First Socially Responsible Investing Portfolio Devoted to Diversity Launched. SocialFunds.com July 31, 2006. - https://www.creativeinvest.com/FirstInvestingPortfolioDevotedtoDiversity.pdf; Black Bank social impact measurement - https://www.creativeinvest.com/BlackBanksNewOrleans.pdf

In addition, Mr. Cunningham has been an active participant in many public policy discussions, having testified before Congress several times. He is also provides expert opinion to Federal Appeals Courts: In May 2021, William Michael Cunningham filed a "Friend of the Court" in City of Oakland vs. Wells Fargo in the US Court of Appeals for the Ninth Circuit. He estimated the damage Wells imposed on Oakland at $12.5 billion.

On June 17, 2015, the US Court of Appeals for the District of Columbia Circuit recognized William Michael Cunningham as a "Friend of the Court" in an action two state securities regulators brought against the US Securities and Exchange Commission (SEC).

In 2012, Mr. Cunningham submitted a "Friend of the Court" brief in the US Court of Appeals for the Second Circuit. The case concerned the rejection, by a Federal Judge, of a settlement agreed to by the US Securities and Exchange Commission (SEC) and Citigroup Global Markets Inc. (Citigroup), the latter accused of securities fraud.

Mr. Cunningham has been involved in the provision of online resources to small businesses for over 26 years, posting his first website in 1995. He graduated from Howard University with a BA in Economics and is a graduate of the University of Chicago Booth School of Business, where he earned his Master of Business Administration degree. Mr. Cunningham also holds a Master's in Economics from the University of Chicago.

Acknowledgments

I would like to thank my college and graduate school interns, current and former, for their help. They are a remarkable group of talented young people. I have been honored to work with them all.

Mr. Andrew Taber, an economics student at Emory University, has been extremely helpful. He worked on this book as part of two summer internships with Creative Investment Research.

Other interns I would like to thank include Ethan Li, American University Washington Mentorship Program, Alice Gabidoulline, University of Michigan, Grace Pottebaum, American University Washington Mentorship Program, Faisal Gbadegbe, Georgetown Law School, Joseph LaRosa, The Ohio State University, Lana Feteiha, Dickinson College, Carlisle, PA; Christopher Moreira, American University Washington Mentorship Program; Amarilis Soler, Florida International University; and Yuyang Zhang, Boston University.

I would also like to thank Armani Jackson at FedEx Office in Maryland for printing early draft chapters for proof reading.

(Of course, any remaining errors and mistakes are mine and mine alone.)

Introduction

This book aims to be a key reference resource for minority businesses and their supporters and customers. We explore and examine current trends, provide a directory of minority business development–related resources, and document new ways minority businesses are thriving. We specifically include relevant information of the recent wave of corporate Black Lives Matter support pledges.

The main topic covered is the current state of minority businesses in the United States. We will look at minority businesses with an optimistic eye.

We explore the positive impact of the dramatic increase in the number of women and minority businesses created in the early 2010s and the increase in the type of firms.

We honestly discuss government contracting, including the Minority Business Development Agency (MBDA), the Offices of Minority and Women Inclusion (OMWI) from Dodd-Frank section 342. Section 342 of the Dodd-Frank Wall Street Reform and Consumer Protection Act contains a "provision creating an Office of Minority and Women Inclusion at various agencies to monitor the diversity efforts of the agencies, the regulated entities and agency contractors."

The book is important because it highlights unused and unrecognized resources at the federal, state, and local levels. There are many national, state, and local organizations focused on minority business development. We list and evaluate these entities.

This book is a "need to have" title because of the comprehensive, objective, and honest advice and information it provides on minority business development (in the midst of the most challenging period for the sector).

The author is one of the longest serving analysts in understanding and analyzing minority business and impact investing trends. His performance is second to none:

- His 2015 presentation at the Texas Association of African American Chambers of Commerce resulted in successful crowdfunding legislation for the State of Texas. See www.creativeinvest.com/TexasEconomicForecastCrowd fundingBill.pdf.

- As he forecast on December 26, 2016, "Under any conceivable scenario, the current situation is very bad, and I mean toxic, for democratic institutions in general and for people of color specifically. Bottom line: our Fully Adjusted Return Forecast** indicates that, over time, things will get much, much worse...." See www.linkedin.com/pulse/trumpism-william-michael-cunningham-am-mba/.

- As he noted on June 11, 2016, "our initial 2016 Election Fully Adjusted Return Forecast indicates that Donald J. Trump will win the election for the Presidency of the United States." See "Why Trump Will Win" at www.linkedin.com/pulse/why-trump-win-william-michael-cunningham-am-mba.

What Readers Will Learn:

- The state of minority business development in the United States

- Relevant and effective resources for minority businesses

- The difference between banks, thrifts, credit unions, angel investors, crowdfunding, venture capital, and how to approach each

- How to create a business plan, how to fill out loan, grant, and credit applications

- How to use social media in support of minority business development goals

- Social media sites and trends: current and relevant minority business–related social media sites and trends

Data files and other relevant information are available for download. The URLs are: https://github.com/Apress/thriving-minority-owned-business and https://www.creativeinvest.com/thriving/.

Minority Business Now

Defining Minority Business

On January 12, 1959, Berry Gordy started Motown Records. The company grew into a global brand and one of the most influential companies in the United States. Mr. Gordy is an African American, born and raised in Detroit, so his firm was considered a "minority business" at its start. It did not remain so. As the firm grew and prospered, the value was recognized. The firm was purchased by MCA Records in 1988. This is widely considered a successful path for a (formerly) minority-owned firm, and if this is your goal, the information contained in this book may very well help you reach it.

Of course, not all minority firms aspire to these heights. Around the same time that Mr. Gordy started his firm, my father, Paul Nicholas Cunningham, started Nicholas Architectural and Construction Co. in Washington DC. The firm grew to be a successful architectural firm, focusing on designing and building Black churches in Washington in the 1960s and 1970s. The firm was profitable enough to allow my father and mother to comfortably raise six children (to the extent that you can ever be comfortable with six children). If this is your goal, this book will definitely help.

© William Michael Cunningham 2021
W. M. Cunningham, *Thriving As a Minority-Owned Business in Corporate America*,
https://doi.org/10.1007/978-1-4842-7240-4_1

This publication aims to be the main reference resource for US-based minority businesses, defined as business firms owned by members of any of the six recognized minority group designations in the United States (Asian (including persons from the Pacific Islands or the Indian Subcontinent), African American (Black), Hispanic and/or Latinx, Multi-ethnic, Native American, and/or Women). The book explores and examines current trends, provides a complete (as of the time of writing) directory of minority business development—related resources, and documents new ways minority businesses are profitably expanding their operating space. The book specifically includes relevant information on the recent wave of corporate support for Black Lives Matter and Black women. We interview successful minority business owners and end by showing that the key to survival is cooperation and collaboration. Our analysis outlines the continuing impacts of COVID-19 and ranks those impacts from most to least significant.

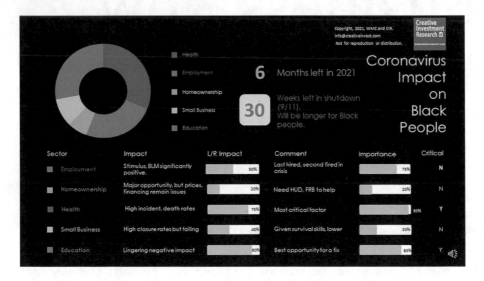

The preceding graphic, from our 2020 research describing the impact of COVID on minority firms, shows that the most critical factor is health: if you are no longer breathing, it really doesn't matter what kind of job or business you have. Of course, if you are still breathing, then your job matters a great deal. Education is next, and it also represents the best opportunity for a fix. By using new technology and techniques, there may be a way to leapfrog the damage done to the educational standing of millions of children and young adults. Small business is next. Finally, homeownership: we believe the Federal Reserve and the Department of Housing and Urban Development will find ways to protect homeowners.[1]

The main subject is the current state of minority businesses in the United States. We define "minority business" in summary earlier and in detail later.

Even in the face of an unprecedented crisis, the book looks at minority businesses with an optimistic eye. We are unabashedly favorable toward minority businesses in general, although skeptical about some "minority business" agencies at the local, state, and federal levels. Minority firms have grown despite these "helpers," not because of them. (Promoters are not the issue: effectiveness is.)

Minority firms boost general economic activity in the United States, often innovating and adding momentum to certain US industries, as Mr. Gordy's experience shows.

This performance continues to the present: from March 24, 2020, to March 24, 2021, a portfolio of stocks in minority banks beat the S&P 500. The S&P 500 Index (green) returned 74.78%. The Minority Bank portfolio (blue) returned 112.27%.

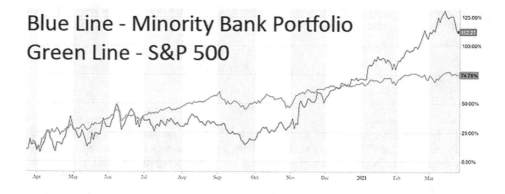

Blue Line - Minority Bank Portfolio
Green Line - S&P 500

---

[1] The Reserve Bank of New Zealand is now "required to consider the impact on housing when making monetary and financial policy decisions: changes have been made to the Central Bank of New Zealand's Monetary Policy Committee's remit requiring it to take into account government policy relating to more sustainable house prices, while working towards its objectives." We think similar policies will be implemented in the United States. See www.beehive.govt.nz/release/reserve-bank-take-account-housing-decision-making

We do not expect this situation to last. Most of the overperformance represented in the preceding graph is due to investments made by large nonminority banks, like JP Morgan, Morgan Stanley, Citibank, and Wells Fargo, into minority banks.[2]

Still, it is a good sign.

We are also optimistic that recent changes in the domestic political environment are good news for minority businesses. The more hopeful approach taken by the new administration means a more rational, fairer approach. One of the first Executive Orders issued by the new administration mandated a "comprehensive approach to advancing equity for all."[3] The order requires the US Government to "identify the best methods, consistent with applicable law, to assist agencies in assessing equity with respect to race, ethnicity, religion, income, geography, gender identity, sexual orientation, and disability." Finally, the order requires that "each agency ... assess whether underserved communities and their members face systemic barriers in accessing benefits and opportunities available" from agency policies and programs. This review is sure to include minority business programs and will lead, hopefully, to greater opportunities.

To place minority business activity in the proper perspective relative to the total economic activity in the United States, the book starts with an examination of the demographic characteristics of the United States as a whole.

---

[2] At the Federal Reserve Bank of Kansas City in 1994, I suggested the Federal Reserve Board's Federal Open Market Committee (FOMC) purchase mortgage-backed securities (MBS) originated by Black banks as part of open market operations. The Fed, then under Alan Greenspan, declined, saying that only Treasury securities were appropriate collateral. Since the financial crisis, the Fed has purchased trillions in securities, helping nonminority banks, broker-dealers, insurance companies, auto companies, and investment banks. Not only did few Black banks receive any assistance, but the ones that did were the wrong banks.

We still believe one possible solution to the crisis is to have the Federal Open Market Committee (FOMC) create a liquidity pool totaling at least $50 billion by conducting repo and reverse repo transactions, purchasing Treasury, MBS securities (and/or SBA PPP loans) from Black banks with a record of actually making loans to the Black community.

We remain confident that, with the increased level of private sector interest as reflected earlier, this is a viable solution.

[3] January 20, 2021. Executive Order On Advancing Racial Equity and Support for Underserved Communities Through the Federal Government. Online at www.whitehouse.gov/briefing-room/presidential-actions/2021/01/20/executive-order-advancing-racial-equity-and-support-for-underserved-communities-through-the-federal-government/

The United States in 2020 and 2024

Population by Gender and Race

Business growth and activity is tied to population growth and activity. As of June 2020, the population of the United States stood at 331,002,651 people according to UN data. The United States represents 4.25% of the total world population.

The US population according to the 2020 Census was estimated to be 331,449,281, an increase from the 2010 Census population estimates of 308,745,538. In 2000, Census estimated the US population at 281,422,025. The best projections estimate that the US population will be 364,072,786 in 2024. While the current crisis will definitely impact these estimates, the outlook for population growth in the United States remains positive.

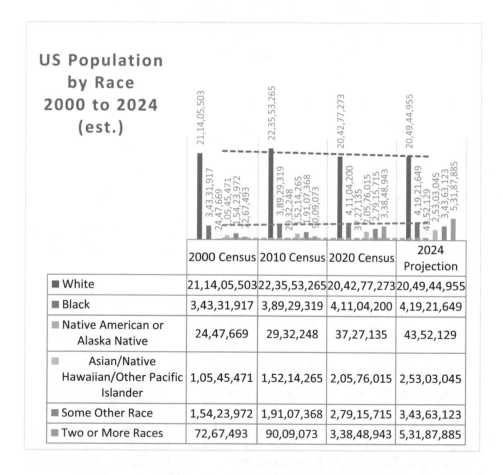

US Population by Race 2000 to 2024 (est.)

	2000 Census	2010 Census	2020 Census	2024 Projection
■ White	21,14,05,503	22,35,53,265	20,42,77,273	20,49,44,955
■ Black	3,43,31,917	3,89,29,319	4,11,04,200	4,19,21,649
■ Native American or Alaska Native	24,47,669	29,32,248	37,27,135	43,52,129
■ Asian/Native Hawaiian/Other Pacific Islander	1,05,45,471	1,52,14,265	2,05,76,015	2,53,03,045
■ Some Other Race	1,54,23,972	1,91,07,368	2,79,15,715	3,43,63,123
■ Two or More Races	72,67,493	90,09,073	3,38,48,943	5,31,87,885

	2000 Census	2010 Census	2020 Census	2024 Projection	Percent Change	
					2000 to 2010	2020 to 2024
Total Population	281,422,025	308,745,538	331,449,281	364,072,786	9.7%	9.8%
Population Density (Pop/Sq Mi)	78.22	87.93	91.54	94.80	12.4%	3.6%
Total Households	105,480,443	116,716,292	125,121,015	130,291,609	10.7%	4.1%

We estimate that 49.2% of the US population was male and 50.8% female, with a median age of 38 years. These factors influence business activity for certain industries and firms. If your firm provides goods and services to women, you will probably want to know the total number of potential customers in your market, even if you never reach all of them. We estimate that there are 91.5 people per square mile in the United States.

US Population by Gender 2000 to 2020						
	2000 Census	%	2010 Census	%	2020 Census Estimates	%
Male	137,907,457	49.0%	151,781,326	49.2%	163,073,046	49.2%
Female	143,514,568	51.0%	156,964,212	50.8%	168,376,235	50.8%

As we noted, depending upon your service, product, industry, and geography, understanding demographic trends in markets that you target will be important.

US Population by Gender: 2024			Percent Change	
	2024 Projections	%	2000 to 2010	2019 to 2024
Male	179,524,291	49.2%	10.1%	10.1%
Female	184,548,495	50.8%	9.4%	9.6%

Since the Census Bureau has not yet issued detailed population estimates by gender and age, the following tables use data from 2019 estimates, not the 2020 Census. In general, these estimates are useful placeholders until the Census Bureau releases updates sometime in late 2021.

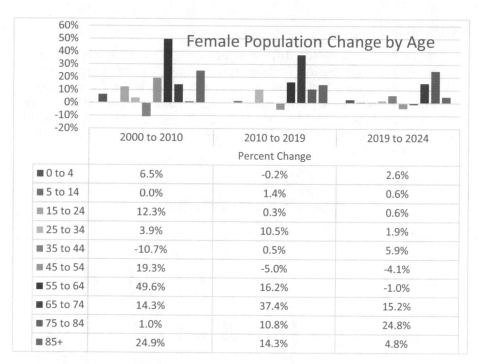

Female Population Change by Age

	2000 to 2010	2010 to 2019	2019 to 2024
		Percent Change	
■ 0 to 4	6.5%	-0.2%	2.6%
■ 5 to 14	0.0%	1.4%	0.6%
■ 15 to 24	12.3%	0.3%	0.6%
■ 25 to 34	3.9%	10.5%	1.9%
■ 35 to 44	-10.7%	0.5%	5.9%
■ 45 to 54	19.3%	-5.0%	-4.1%
■ 55 to 64	49.6%	16.2%	-1.0%
■ 65 to 74	14.3%	37.4%	15.2%
■ 75 to 84	1.0%	10.8%	24.8%
■ 85+	24.9%	14.3%	4.8%

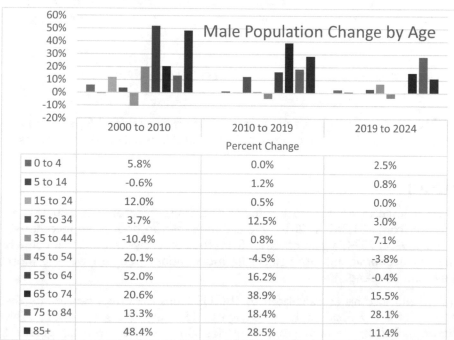

Male Population Change by Age

	2000 to 2010	2010 to 2019	2019 to 2024
		Percent Change	
■ 0 to 4	5.8%	0.0%	2.5%
■ 5 to 14	-0.6%	1.2%	0.8%
■ 15 to 24	12.0%	0.5%	0.0%
■ 25 to 34	3.7%	12.5%	3.0%
■ 35 to 44	-10.4%	0.8%	7.1%
■ 45 to 54	20.1%	-4.5%	-3.8%
■ 55 to 64	52.0%	16.2%	-0.4%
■ 65 to 74	20.6%	38.9%	15.5%
■ 75 to 84	13.3%	18.4%	28.1%
■ 85+	48.4%	28.5%	11.4%

Households

One key metric is *households*, defined as one or more people who share the same housing unit. For business selling products that provide services to more than one person, cars, for example, keeping track of these factors may be important. We estimate that there are 125,121,015 households in the United States, up from 116,716,292 households in 2010, and up from 105,480,443 in 2000. We estimate the number of households in the United States will be 130,291,609 in 2024.

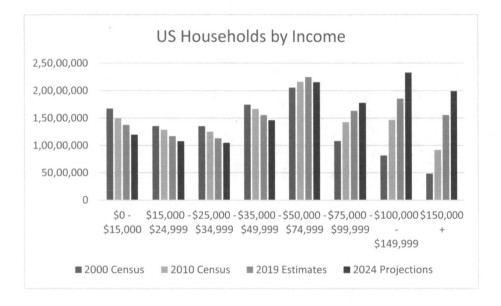

In 2010, on average, US citizens spent 12.9 years living with 2.6 people in the same property. The average family consisted of 3.2 people and 1.9 vehicles.

Income

In 2019, median household income in the United States was $60,811, an increase from $51,362 in 2010. We estimate median household income will be $69,997 in 2024, a gain of 15.1% from the current year. Median income is one key economic indicator, since the more money people have, the more they tend to spend.

Household income as calculated by the US Census Bureau represents the income of every resident over the age of 15 living in a given house. This metric includes pre-tax wages and salaries, along with any pre-tax personal business, investment, or other recurring sources of income, as well as any kind of governmental entitlement such as unemployment insurance, social security, disability payments, or child support payments received.

In 2019, US per capita income was $28,088, while 2019 average household income totaled $33,623.

Median income "divides the US income distribution into two equal groups, half having income above that amount, and half having income below that amount." In the case of a heavily unequal distribution, median income overestimates fairness, that is, it makes the economic situation appear fairer than it is. To get a better picture, we should use other indicators for US households with positive incomes, since the mode (most frequent income) for US individuals is likely to be zero. This is due to the large number of elderly, children, and students in the US population.

Race and Ethnicity

Many, but not all, minority businesses start by selling goods and services to persons in the same ethnic group as the owners of the firm. Motown started selling records that specifically appealed to African Americans, for example. Having an understanding of general minority and ethnic population trends will be important to you if this product and service sales strategy applies to your firm.

In 2020, the population of the United States was 61.6% White (alone), 12.4% Black (alone), 1% Native American, 6% Asian (alone), and 0.2% Pacific Islander. Eight percent (actually, 8.4%) of all 2020 Census respondents self-classified as belonging to Some Other Race alone.

■ **Note**   The 2020 Census also allowed respondents to select the category "in combination" for each racial grouping. The Census Bureau uses three categories to discuss race:

Race alone – Membership in one racial category

Race in combination – Membership in more than one racial group

Race alone or in combination, adding data from the preceding two categories.

The following chart displays general trends. Note that the White (alone) population, still the largest race or ethnicity group in the United States, decreased by 8.6% from 2010. This decline should be placed in context, however. While the White alone population category declined, the White in combination population category increased by 316%.

This means that as the country racially diversifies, so does its largest population group.

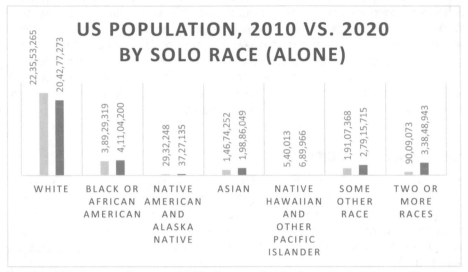

Source: US Census Bureau, 2010 Census Public Law Redistricting Data File (P.L. 94-171) Summary File; 2020 Census Public Law Redistricting Data File (P.L. 94-171) Summary File

In tabular form:

US Population by Race	2010		
	Alone	In combination	Alone or in combination
White	223,553,265	7,487,133	231,040,398
Black or African American	38,929,319	3,091,424	42,020,743
Native American and Alaska Native	2,932,248	2,288,331	5,220,579
Asian	14,674,252	2,646,604	17,320,856
Native Hawaiian and Other Pacific Islander	540,013	685,182	1,225,195
Some Other Race	19,107,368	2,640,716	21,748,084
Two or More Races	9,009,073	N/M	N/M
	2020		
White	204,277,273	31,134,234	235,411,507
Black or African American	41,104,200	5,832,533	46,936,733
American Indian and Alaska Native	3,727,135	5,938,923	9,666,058
Asian	19,886,049	4,114,949	24,000,998
Native Hawaiian and Other Pacific Islander	689,966	896,497	1,586,463
Some Other Race	27,915,715	21,986,821	49,902,536
Two or More Races	33,848,943	N/M	N/M

Source: US Census Bureau, 2010 Census Public Law Redistricting Data File (P.L. 94-171) Summary File; 2020 Census Public Law Redistricting Data File (P.L. 94-171) Summary File
N/M = Not meaningful.

The following chart describes the US population by race, but focuses on combinations. The increase in the multiracial population was especially notable and may point to the future for the United States as a multiracial country. This development has definite implications for minority business development in the coming years.

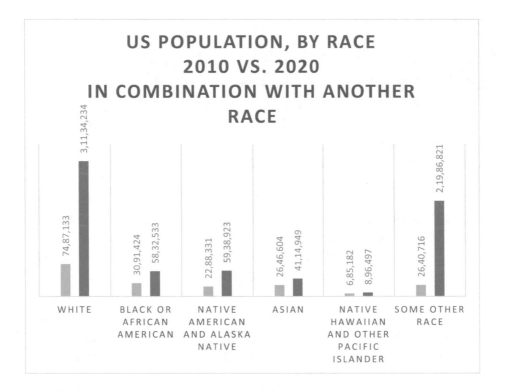

US POPULATION, BY RACE 2010 VS. 2020 IN COMBINATION WITH ANOTHER RACE

These racial categories can be confusing, so we have provided the following definitions. Understand that the goal of this methodology is to generate more accurate estimates of the minority population in the United States.

Definitions White alone – White alone refers to people who reported White and did not report any other race category.

White alone or in combination – White alone or in combination consists of those respondents who reported White, whether or not they reported any other races. In other words, people who reported only White or who reported combinations such as "White and Black or African American" or "White and Asian and American Indian and Alaska Native" are included in the White alone or in combination category.

Black alone – Black alone refers to people who reported Black or African American and did not report any other race.

Black alone or in combination – Black alone or in combination consists of those respondents who reported Black, whether or not they reported any other races. In other words, people who reported only Black or who reported combinations such as "Black and White" or "Black and Asian and American Indian and Alaska Native" are included in the Black alone or in combination category.

AIAN alone – AIAN alone refers to people who reported American Indian and Alaska Native and did not report any other race.

AIAN alone or in combination – AIAN alone or in combination consists of those respondents who reported American Indian and/or Alaska Native, whether or not they reported any other races. In other words, people who reported only AIAN or who reported combinations such as "AIAN and White" or "AIAN and Black and Asian" are included in the AIAN alone or in combination category.

Asian alone – Asian alone refers to people who reported Asian and did not report any other race.

Asian alone or in combination – Asian alone or in combination consists of those respondents who reported Asian, whether or not they reported any other races. In other words, people who reported only Asian or who reported combinations such as "Asian and White" or "Asian and Black and NHOPI" are included in the Asian alone or in combination category.

NHOPI alone – NHOPI alone refers to people who reported Native Hawaiian or Other Pacific Islander and did not report any other race.

NHOPI alone or in combination – NHOPI alone or in combination consists of those respondents who reported Native Hawaiian or Other Pacific Islander, whether or not they reported any other races. In other words, people who reported only NHOPI or who reported combinations such as "NHOPI and White" or "NHOPI and Black and Asian" are included in the NHOPI alone or in combination category.

Asian/NHOPI alone – Asian/NHOPI alone refers to people who reported Asian or Native Hawaiian or Other Pacific Islander and did not report any other race.

Asian/NHOPI alone or in combination – Asian/NHOPI alone or in combination consists of those respondents who reported Asian or Native Hawaiian or Other Pacific Islander, whether or not they reported any other races. In other words, people who reported only Asian or NHOPI or who reported combinations such as "NHOPI and White" or "NHOPI and Black and Asian" are included in the Asian/NHOPI alone or in combination category.

Two or More Races – This category represents all those respondents who reported more than one race.

From: www.census.gov/programs-surveys/cps/data/data-tools/cps-table-creator-help/race-definitions.html

The following chart describes the US population by race, alone or in combination. Note that, under this definition, the White population increased:

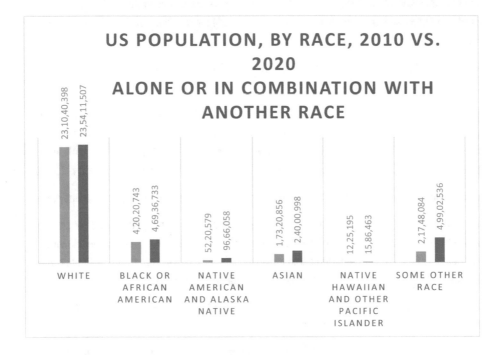

Data on the Hispanic or Latino Population

Based on the 2020 Census, we determined that the Hispanic or Latino population increased to 62.1 million (18.7%) of the US population in 2020, up from 50.5 million (16.3%) in 2010. We note that 51% of the growth in the US population between 2010 and 2020 was due to the growth in the Hispanic or Latino population.

In percentage terms:

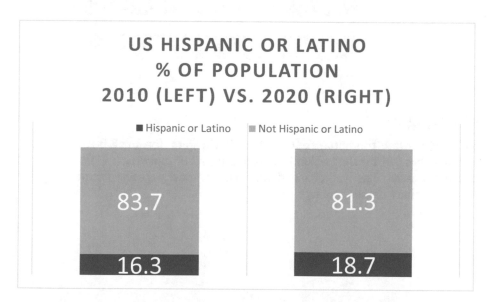

Clearly, this trend has definite implications for minority business development and growth in the United States. It will influence the allocation of minority business development resources (loans, grants) at the state and local levels. It may also influence your need or desire to become a Spanish speaker, if you are not already, in order to better communicate with employees, customers, and policy makers.

Note that Hispanics are considered an ethnicity and are counted independently of race,[4] since you can be Black and Hispanic, White and Hispanic, etc. People of Hispanic origin represent 18.2% of the US population.

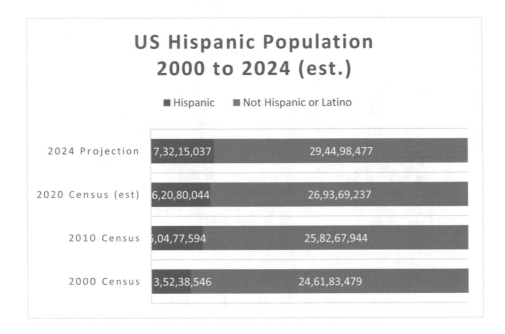

US Hispanic Population 2000 to 2024 (est.)

■ Hispanic   ■ Not Hispanic or Latino

	Hispanic	Not Hispanic or Latino
2024 Projection	7,32,15,037	29,44,98,477
2020 Census (est)	6,20,80,044	26,93,69,237
2010 Census	5,04,77,594	25,82,67,944
2000 Census	3,52,38,546	24,61,83,479

Housing

Housing is often the initial source of startup capital for small businesses, so keeping track of housing valuation trends may be important. Unfortunately, homeownership has not changed for many minority group members. The following chart details this fact.

---

[4] According to the US Census Bureau, "It is important to note that these data comparisons between the 2020 Census and 2010 Census race data should be made with caution, taking into account the improvements we have made to the Hispanic origin and race questions and the ways we code what people tell us." From www.census.gov/library/stories/2021/08/improved-race-ethnicity-measures-reveal-united-states-population-much-more-multiracial.html

The percentage of U.S. blacks who own their own homes today is the same as when housing discrimination was outlawed in 1968. The 1970 census found 42% of black households owned their own homes. In 2017, the number was 41%.

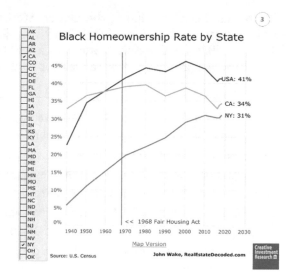

Black Homeownership Rate by State

USA: 41%
CA: 34%
NY: 31%

<< 1968 Fair Housing Act

Map Version

Source: U.S. Census

John Wake, RealEstateDecoded.com

Creative Investment Research ℤ

In addition, the pandemic left Black homeowners and renters in a precarious state as described in the following chart. It shows that, of 2.7 million Black renters or homeowners, 1.2 million say they are somewhat or very likely to face foreclosure or eviction. (Source: http://Census.gov). Week 30 Household Pulse Survey: May 12–May 24.

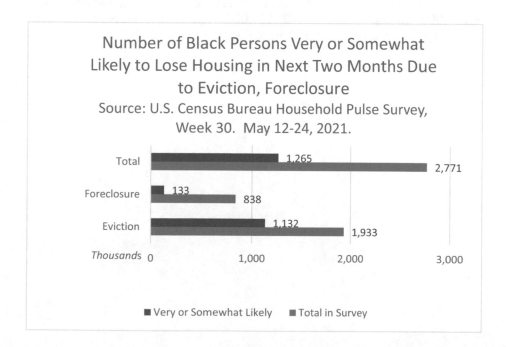

Number of Black Persons Very or Somewhat Likely to Lose Housing in Next Two Months Due to Eviction, Foreclosure

Source: U.S. Census Bureau Household Pulse Survey, Week 30. May 12-24, 2021.

- Total: 1,265 / 2,771
- Foreclosure: 133 / 838
- Eviction: 1,132 / 1,933

Thousands

- ■ Very or Somewhat Likely
- ■ Total in Survey

The median housing value in the United States was $110,813 in 2000; the estimated median housing value in 2019 was $212,058. The average rent in 2019 was $824 for the United States as a whole. In rapidly gentrifying urban areas, however, average rents are well above this figure.

■ **Note** "From 2007 to 2009, household wealth, with and without home equity, dropped sharply for black and white families. But during the crucial recovery period of 2009 to 2011, black and white families had very different experiences. In that period, white wealth levels, excluding home equity, began to show signs of recovery: median white household wealth exhibited zero loss. During that same time period, however, black households continued to experience severe declines, with the typical black household losing 40 percent of non-home-equity wealth." From: Impact of the US Housing Crisis on the Racial Wealth Gap Across Generations. S Burd-Sharps, R Rasch. Online at www.aclu.org/sites/default/files/field_document/discrimlend_final.pdf

---

Employment

As with the size of the industry you are in, understanding general employment trends may help you estimate employment costs. As unemployment falls, wages, in general, rise. In July 2019, 157,346,000 persons over the age of 16 were in the labor force. By July 2020, this had fallen to 143,532,000 employed, 16,338,000 unemployed, and 100,503,000 not in the labor force. The percentage of Americans in the Armed Forces remains 0.6%.

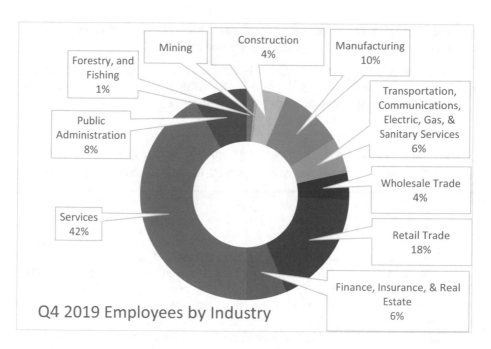

Q4 2019 Employees by Industry

To understand where your business fits in the general business environment and to understand how many potential competitors you might have, it is critical to know the size, generally, of the industry your firm operates in. By the fourth quarter of 2019, there were an estimated 12,162,901 business establishments in the United States. White-collar workers made up 60.6% of the population, and blue-collar occupations made up 20.9%. Service and Farm workers made up 18.4% of the population.

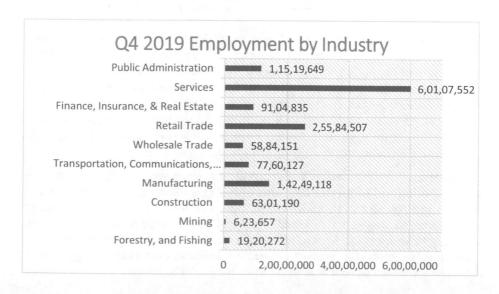

In 2018, the US average, one-way commute time was 26.1 minutes. In 2010, the average time traveled to work was 28 minutes.

*Establishment counts include D&B business location records that have a valid telephone, known SIC code, and D&B rating as well as exclude cottage industries (businesses that operate from a residence).

■ **Note** We will explore the positive impact of the dramatic increase in the number of women and minority businesses that were created in the early 2010s and the increase in the type of firms.

Defining *"Minority"*

The United Nations Minorities Declaration of 1992 offers an internationally agreed-upon definition of who is considered a minority. According to the declaration, reproduced as follows, minorities are people with national or ethnic, cultural, religious, or linguistic identities, whose existence should be protected by the State. A common characteristic of a minority group is a nondominant position in political, social, and economic matters due to ethnic, cultural, religious, or linguistic differences relative to the majority population in a given State.

■ **Note** Declaration on the Rights of Persons Belonging to National or Ethnic, Religious and Linguistic Minorities. Adopted by General Assembly resolution 47/135 of 18 December 1992. (www.ohchr.org/EN/ProfessionalInterest/Pages/Minorities.aspx)

Discrimination against minorities based on religion may be a bigger concern in other countries. For example, Buddhists represent the overwhelming religious majority in Burma. Individuals who do not follow this faith have reported significant discrimination in the form of denied permits or licenses. Religious discrimination has long been a serious issue. Turkey experienced the Armenian, Greek, and Assyrian Genocides, for example. Western cultures, and those following these cultures, have a tendency to persecute groups based on religious identity.

Gender-based discrimination is also significant, since women also experience discrimination and often face the same challenges minority-owned businesses do, like lack of access to equal credit opportunities. A Boston Consulting Group analysis suggests that equal entrepreneurial participation on the part of men and women would result in a 2.5 to 5 trillion-dollar increase in global GDP. This suggests that growth in women business entrepreneurship would result in increased potential economic activity on a global scale.

The recognition of minority businesses in the United States differs from the broader definition of minorities adopted by the United Nations. The US Minority Business Development Agency (MBDA) differentiates minority business enterprises based on ethnic or national identities. This is due to the history of discrimination against ethnic minorities that has occurred throughout the country's history and that continues to persist today.

What Is a Minority Business Enterprise?

The term "Minority Business Enterprise (MBE)" refers to any business in the United States that is more than 50% owned or controlled by African Americans, Asian Americans, Hispanic Americans, Native Americans, Women, or a combination thereof. (This definition has been expanded, in some places, to include persons with certain religious, disability, or sexual orientation characteristics. We provide a list of these expanded categories later in this chapter.)

As of April 2017, there were 8 million minority-owned businesses in the United States, a 38% increase from the previous decade.

The Minority Business Development Agency (MBDA) is an agency within the US Department of Commerce that supports the growth and development of minority-owned businesses through various programs, policies, and access to capital. These efforts are meant to better prepare minority businesses to grow, expand, and function efficiently. The main functions of the MBDA are global business development, access to capital and financial management, access to contracts, access to markets, and strategic business consulting.

MBDA also found that of the $1.3 trillion minority business market segment, only 11% of firms have paid employees. This demonstrates that a significant portion of minority businesses are sole proprietors.

Minority-owned firms are important because of their enhanced entrepreneurial return and benefits. They add significant value to the employment market, invest in their communities, and bring innovation to the nation.

A significant issue regarding MBEs is that while they are representative of overall economic prosperity, it is also often more difficult for them to receive the capital required for growth. According to the MBDA, "They are more likely to receive lower loan amounts, pay higher interest rates, or be denied funding altogether." This is a critical issue that we will discuss in subsequent chapters.

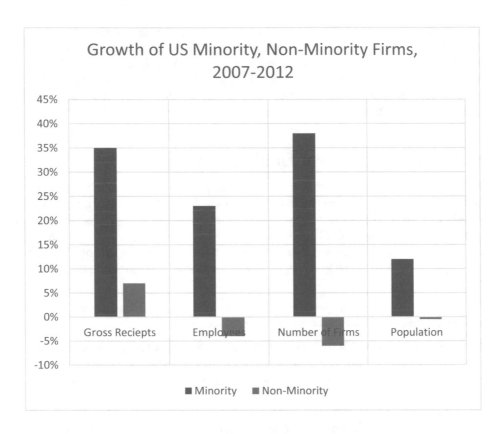

Growth of US Minority, Non-Minority Firms, 2007-2012

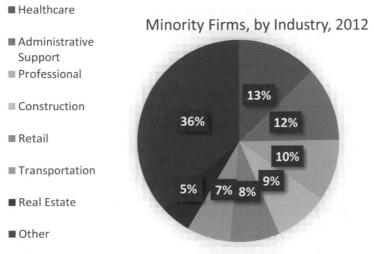

Minority Firms, by Industry, 2012

Minority Business Categories

The earliest Federal programs to assist minority businesses were created by executive orders, starting with President Franklin Roosevelt's order on June 25, 1941, requiring federal agencies to include a clause in defense-related contracts prohibiting government contractors from discriminating on the basis of "race, creed, color, or national origin." This order was focused on providing employment opportunities for African Americans, not on supporting minority businesses.

The Kerner Commission Report on the causes of the 1966 urban riots "concluded that African Americans would need 'special encouragement' to enter the economic mainstream." While this ignored the core systemic racism that prevented Blacks from creating companies and from generating wealth, it was the spur for the development of all modern minority business programs.

The systemic racism noted earlier is still prevalent today: while federal government agencies are supposed to provide financial incentives to private and public sector companies that do a certain amount of business with minority-owned enterprises, this effort has been ineffective. Several factors have led to this outcome.

According to the US SBA, 8(a) firms receiving contracts from the Federal Government totaled 3871 in FY 2019.[5] This compares to the total 4 million minority firms in the United States. Under any circumstance, this program must be regarded as ineffective except in very narrow circumstances. If you are a former Federal government employee or if you are looking for contracts in certain very narrowly defined areas (for African Americans, these include security guard or janitorial services), then these programs may work. Otherwise…no. In fact, recently released data shows that Black owned firms received 1.67% of Federal contracting dollars in FY2020.

---

[5] SBA FY 2021 Congressional Justification and FY 2019 Annual Performance Report. Total Number of Minority Firms from US Senate Small Business Committee. www.sbc.senate. gov/public/index.cfm/minorityentrepreneurs

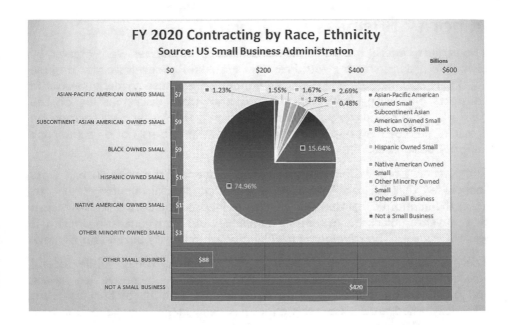

We discuss these factors in a later chapter.

As the benefits from minority business programs at the Federal level grew, other minority groups demanded consideration. Today, a long list of business owner characteristics is eligible for certification as a minority business:

- Small Business Administration 8a Program (SBA 8 (a))
- Alaska Native Claims (ANC)
- Certified Small Business (CSB)
- Disabled Business Enterprise (DIS)
- Disabled Veteran Business Enterprise (DVET)
- Disadvantaged Business Enterprise (DBE)
- Disadvantaged Veteran Enterprise (DVE)
- Green Certified (Green)
- Historically Black College/University (HBCU/MI)
- HUBZone Certified (HUBZONE)
- Labor Surplus Jurisdiction (LSA)
- Minority-Owned Business Enterprise (MBE)
- Minority Owned – African American
- Minority Owned – Asian Pacific
- Minority Owned – Hispanic
- Minority Owned – Indian Subcontinent
- Minority Owned – Native American
- Service-Disabled Veteran (SDV)
- Small Business Enterprise (SBE)
- Small Disadvantaged Business Enterprise (SDB)
- Veteran-Owned Business Enterprise (VET)
- Veteran Owned (VBE)
- Vietnam Veteran Owned (VVET)
- Woman-Owned Business Enterprise (WBE)
- Woman Owned (MWBE)

Additional Minority Business Designations

Small Business Administration 8a Program (SBA 8 (a))
Alaska Native Claims (ANC)
Certified Small Business (CSB)
Disabled Business Enterprise (DIS)
Disabled Veteran Business Enterprise (DVET)
Disadvantaged Business Enterprise (DBE)
Disadvantaged Veteran Enterprise (DVE)
Green Certified (Green)
Historically Black College/University (HBCU/MI)
HUBZone Certified (HUBZONE)
Labor Surplus Jurisdiction (LSA)
Minority-Owned Business Enterprise (MBE)
Minority Owned – African American
Minority Owned – Asian Pacific
Minority Owned – Hispanic
Minority Owned – Indian Subcontinent
Minority Owned – Native American
Service-Disabled Veteran (SDV)
Small Business Enterprise (SBE)
Small Disadvantaged Business Enterprise (SDB)
Veteran-Owned Business Enterprise (VET)
Veteran Owned (VBE)
Vietnam Veteran Owned (VVET)
Woman-Owned Business Enterprise (WBE)
Woman Owned (MWBE)

These categories are defined as follows.

Alaska Native Claims

Section 450b(e) of title 25 U.S.C. "Indian tribe" means any Indian tribe, band, nation, or other organized group or community, including any Alaska Native village or regional or village corporation as defined in or established pursuant to the Alaska Native Claims Settlement Act (85 Stat. 688) (43 U.S.C. 1601 et seq.), which is recognized as eligible for the special programs and services provided by the United States to Indians because of their status as Indians.

Certified Small Business

Indicates whether the business is small and one which has been certified by a federal, state, or local government agency or organization as having met all of the government standards that award eligibility.

Disabled Business Enterprise

At least 51% owned and controlled by a handicapped individual or service-disabled individual. A handicapped individual is a person with a physical, mental, or emotional impairment, defect, ailment, disease, or disability of a permanent nature, which any way limits the selection of any type of employment for which the individual(s) would otherwise be qualified or qualifiable.

Disabled Veteran Business Enterprise

At least 51% owned and controlled by one or more disabled veterans. The home office must be located in the United States, and the home office cannot be a branch or subsidiary of a non-US corporation, firm, or other non-US-based business. The individual(s) must be a veteran of US military services and has a service-connected disability of at least 10% or more.

Disadvantaged Business Enterprise

As defined by the US Department of Transportation. At least 51% owned and controlled by individual(s) who are socially and economically disadvantaged as defined by the DBE Regulation 49 CFR Parts 23 and 26. All eligible owners must certify they are members of a disadvantaged group (eligible ethnic group and/or female). Additionally, the owner(s)' assets cannot exceed $750,000, excluding the assets of the business seeking the DBE certification and the owner(s)' primary residence.

Disadvantaged Veteran Enterprise

A business that is a small business concern owned and controlled by veterans, where not less than 51% is owned, controlled, and managed by veterans. As defined in (38 U.S.C. 101(2)). See the veteran definition.

Gay, Lesbian, Bisexual, and Transgender

A business that is at least 51% owned by a gay, lesbian, bisexual, or transgender entrepreneur, and certified by the National Gay & Lesbian Chamber of Commerce.

Green Certified

A business that is certified by an agency as having met all of their standards for award eligibility within one of the following categories: process, product, building, design, energy, food, community, and tourism.

Historically Black College/University

Postsecondary academic institutions founded before 1964 whose educational mission has historically been the education of Black Americans.

Historically Underutilized Business Zone

As defined by the US SBA HUBZone Empowerment Program. Qualifying businesses must meet small business size criteria and must be located in distressed areas.

Labor Surplus Jurisdiction

Labor Surplus is generally defined for a Civil Jurisdiction rather than the entire MSA (Metropolitan Statistical Area) where the average unemployment number is 20% higher than the average US unemployment rate in the last two calendar years.

Minority-Owned Business Enterprise

At least 51% owned and controlled by individuals belonging to one or more of the following US Federal Government identified ethnic groups: Asian, African American, Hispanic, Asian Indian, Asian Pacific, Native American, Alaska Native.

Small Business Administration 8a Program

At least 51% owned and controlled by socially and economically disadvantaged individual(s). Under the Small Business Act, presumed groups include African Americans, Hispanic Americans, Asian Pacific Americans, Subcontinent Asian Americans, and Native Americans. Other individuals can be admitted to the program if they demonstrate through "the preponderance of the evidence" that they are disadvantaged because of race, ethnicity, gender, physical handicap, or residence in an environment isolated from the mainstream of American society. In order to meet the economic disadvantage test, all individuals must have a net worth of less than $250,000, excluding the value of the subject business and the owner(s)' primary residence.

Service-Disabled Veteran

A business owned by a veteran with a disability that is service connected. The term "service connected" means, with respect to disability or death, that such disability was incurred or aggravated, in the line of duty in the active military, naval, or air service (38 U.S.C. 101(16)).

Small Business Enterprise

Businesses smaller than a specified size (within an industry) as measured by its employee size and/or revenue. These criteria are defined in the US SBA Regulations, 13 CFR Part 121.

Small Disadvantaged Business Enterprise

At least 51% owned and controlled by socially and economically disadvantaged individual(s). African Americans, Hispanic Americans, Asian Pacific Americans, Subcontinent Asian Americans, and Native Americans are presumed to qualify. Other individuals qualify if they show a "preponderance of the evidence" that they are disadvantaged. All individuals must have a net worth of less than $750,000, excluding the equity of the business and primary residence. Successful applications must also meet the SBA small business requirements as defined earlier.

Veteran-Owned Business Enterprise

At least 51% owned and controlled by US citizens who are veterans of the US military service.

Veteran Owned

A business that is at least 51% owned by one or more veterans, who control and operate the business. Control in this context means exercising the power to make policy decisions, and operate means to be actively involved in the day-to-day management of the business. The term "veteran" (38 U.S.C. 101(2)) means a person who served in the active military, naval, or air service and who was discharged or released there.

Vietnam Veteran Owned

A business that is at least 51% owned by one or more Vietnam veterans who served between January 1, 1959 and May 7, 1975 and control and operate the business. Control in this context means exercising the power to make policy decisions, and operate means to be actively involved in the day-to-day management of the business.

Woman-Owned Business Enterprise

At least 51% owned and controlled by individuals who are female.

Minority/Woman-Owned Business

At least 51% owned and controlled by individuals belonging to certain ethnic minority groups and/or who are female in gender. This category is used when the data source does not specify the gender/minority classification, only that the business is one or the other.

This has diluted the impact minority business programs have on the group they were originally intended to benefit: African Americans. This has been reflective of the economic benefits of these programs, especially in markets where small firms face increasing competition from larger and larger firms. As income inequality has worsened, those who are bearing the brunt of this factor have often sought to become certified minority-owned businesses. Further, as the importance of this designation has grown, so has a "minority business certification" industry. This has, paradoxically, increased the importance of accreditation via a respected certification program. With the general growth and adoption of new technology, however, many alternative minority business certification platforms are available.

The State of Minority Business

Challenges and Opportunities

On December 26, 2016, I made the following forecast:

> *Under any conceivable scenario, the current situation is very bad, and I mean toxic, for democratic institutions in general and for people of color specifically. Bottom line: our Fully Adjusted Return Forecast** indicates that, over time, things will get much, much worse.*[1]

Now, we will be the first to admit that we did not have this specific global pandemic in mind when we made this forecast. The economic crisis we now face is without precedent. This does not, however, mean it was unforeseen. Our analysis featured an honest review of recent history in a way that others

---

[1] From *Trumpism.*
www.linkedin.com/pulse/trumpism-william-michael-cunningham-am-mba/

© William Michael Cunningham 2021
W. M. Cunningham, *Thriving As a Minority-Owned Business in Corporate America*,
https://doi.org/10.1007/978-1-4842-7240-4_2

did not, including the fact that "uneducated white Americans are living sicker and dying earlier" due to 40 years of sustained economic turmoil. These facts were combined with standard financial and investment analysis, with a specific focus on management competence. (After all, putting the owner of a small hot dog stand in charge of the largest hot dog manufacturer in the United States probably will not work out well.)

Clearly, demand for goods and services has fallen. Unemployment has increased dramatically. These impacts are global in nature and will be with us for some time. This crisis has impacted Black and minority-owned firms especially hard, as we describe in the following.

Still, even in the face of these facts, we believe there are significant opportunities. Before we get to these, however, we will set the stage with a review data on the current state of minority businesses in the United States. Uncovering those opportunities will require a hard, cold review of the facts.

■ **Quote** "I have great respect for the past. If you don't know where you've come from, you don't know where you're going. I have respect for the past, but I'm a person of the moment. I'm here, and I do my best to be completely centered at the place I'm at, then I go forward to the next place." Maya Angelou Quotes. *From: BrainyQuote.com, BrainyMedia Inc, 2020.* www.brainyquote.com/quotes/maya_angelou_634505, *accessed August 16, 2020.*

Our review is nontraditional: in order to be able to forecast as accurately as we did on December 26, 2016, we have found that we must look at things from a different perspective. So it is here. While the impact the COVID-19 crisis on the broader economy tends to be reflected by mainstream media as hitting the real estate and stock markets especially hard, we focus on its impact on the human beings who own and operate small businesses. We do so by using new data sources. In this way, we can avoid the trap that confuses most economists, who are often befuddled by a "lack of timely business-level data released by the government." We use information from social media–based resources.

I will understand if you are suspicious and skeptical, but bear with me.

The United States in 2024: General and Minority Population Growth Rates

Overall, demographic data suggests that the US economy remains strong. The country's population is expected to grow by 3.2%, from 329 million in 2019 to 339 million by 2024. Over the long term, the age distribution of the country will be bolstered by long term demographic trends, including the anticipated recovery of the population following the COVID crisis.

■ **Quote** "Demography is destiny." Auguste Comte. We review demographics because the impact of population change on economic activity is profound. Consider, for example, the economic and social implications of an aging population. While demographic changes arrive slowly, their effects are overpowering.

Minority populations in the United States continue to grow, boding well for minority business firms. Changes in employment, while challenging, will provide some support for existing and older minority firms seeking to expand their headcount. Income should rebound following a decline, but distribution remains an issue. Firms that focus on providing value for consumers in the lower-income categories, and firms that shift their product offerings to appeal to customers in these sectors, should do well.

We describe and outline several of these factors in the following. This data does not match the population data in Chapter 1 because it represents a forecast to 2024 from another source.

	2019 Estimates	2024 Projections	Percentage Change 2019 to 2024
Total Population	329,329,799	339,726,741	3.2%
Total Households	125,121,015	130,166,520	4.0%
Population by Gender:			
Male	162,193,543	167,519,256	3.5%
Female	167,136,256	172,207,485	3.2%

Total population growth is expected to decline from a 2019 projected rate of 3.5% to a 3.2% rate as estimated in 2020, the impact of slower economic growth due to the COVID crisis.

COVID's Impact

The following chart shows the differential impact of COVID by race. It describes the elevated impact the disease has had on the minority community, relative to whites.

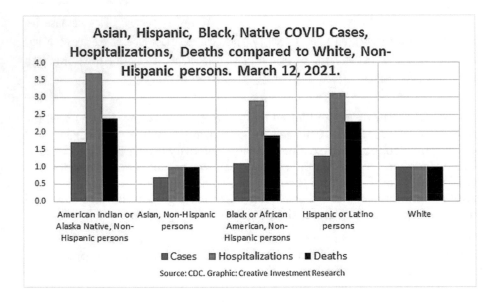

Source: CDC. Graphic: Creative Investment Research

Age Distribution

The distribution of the population by age has implications for minority firms. We discuss these as follows.

Age Distribution of the US Population, 2019 to 2024				
	2019 Estimates	Distribution	**2024 Projections**	Distribution
0 to 4	20,176,621	6.1%	27,415,948	8.1%
5 to 14	41,559,682	12.6%	42,689,383	12.6%
15 to 19	21,385,386	6.5%	28,251,336	8.3%
20 to 24	22,415,222	6.8%	29,102,691	8.6%
25 to 34	45,781,437	13.9%	46,720,580	13.8%
35 to 44	41,335,302	12.6%	43,856,004	12.9%
45 to 54	42,869,957	13.0%	37,616,583	11.1%
55 to 64	42,405,076	12.9%	35,147,109	10.3%
65 to 74	29,982,277	9.1%	27,657,833	8.1%
75 to 84	14,887,459	4.5%	15,324,394	4.5%
85+	6,531,380	2.0%	5,945,218	1.8%

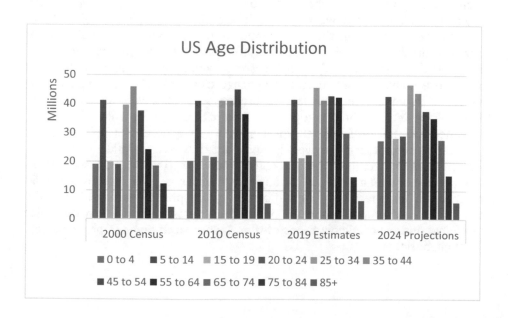

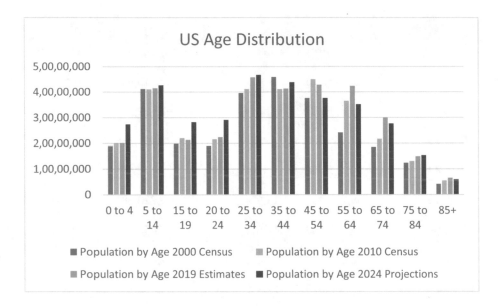

We expect an increase in the population of 0- to 4-year-olds, given the 2020 lockdown. The population in the 5- to 14-year-old cohort should increase. Of course, we expect the crisis to have negative impacts in older demographic categories, especially for minority group members.

Carefully consider the age group most likely to utilize your product or service, then examine the total number of persons in your targeted age group. If your product is of universal appeal regardless of age, fine. But, if not, these numbers tell you something about the total number of persons who may be eligible to buy your product. Do you sell age-restricted products, like cannabis, wine, or tobacco? Check the totals. Are you focused on young adults? Parents? Observe how these numbers are projected to change over time. This is simply a way to begin to understand the factors driving sales at a very disaggregated, 40,000-foot level. Ethnic, geographic, and other factors will, of course, influence your business at a very local level, but, in general, not only will your business be subject to these overall trends, but these trends influence demand for products and services that are complementary to yours. For example, if the number of young adults of car buying age declines, your tire business will be affected. Yes, there are, as I said before, geographic differences, but since cars are manufactured based on national averages, minority firms should carefully consider the implications of these age-related demographic changes for their business.

Race

The trend toward racial diversity is continuing. This bodes well for minority-owned firms: customers in core minority categories will increase. As we noted in an article on the Diversity Fund, "in an environment, a culture, and an economy that is getting more diverse all the time, the diverse company is going to have more customers, and this should lead to higher revenue and higher profits, assuming their costs are under control. They should do better over the long term than the non-diverse company."[2]

Of course, minority firms do not just serve minority customers, but generalized support from persons sharing demographic characteristics with minority business owners will, we anticipate, have a positive impact for these firms overall.[3]

We discuss the limits of this generalized support in subsequent chapters.

Population by Race	2019 Estimates	2024 Projections	Percentage Change, 2019 to 2024
White	230,748,569	234,252,717	1.5%
Black	42,369,857	43,604,356	2.9%
American Indian or Alaska Native	3,232,737	3,337,714	3.2%
Asian/Native Hawaiian/Other Pacific Islander	19,279,970	21,303,045	10.5%
Some Other Race	22,427,331	24,483,062	9.2%
Two or More Races	11,271,335	12,745,847	13.1%

These growth rates, while positive, have fallen from growth estimates made in 2019 due to 2019's slower economic activity. The point is that the growth in diversity is projected to slow, so if your product or service depends upon growing numbers of minority customers, this may impact your plan and revenue. These are national averages, so trends may be differing significantly in your specific geographic area. The industry in which you operate will also have an impact on strategy and potential.

---

[2] See William Michael Cunningham on Impact Investing, Blockchain, and Crowdfunding. November 08, 2018. Online at www.impactinvesting.online/2018/11/william-michael-cunningham-on-impact.html
[3] See http://diversityfund.net

Population by Race	Percent Change	
	2000 to 2010	2019 to 2024
White	5.7%	1.5%
Black	13.4%	2.9%
American Indian or Alaska Native	19.8%	3.2%
Asian/Native Hawaiian/Other Pacific Islander	44.3%	10.5%
Some Other Race	23.9%	9.2%
Two or More Races	24.0%	13.1%

The preceding chart shows the US population by race from 2000 to 2024.

Overall, racial diversity in the United States will continue to increase, led by Asian population projected growth of 10.5% from 2019 to 2024.

Ethnicity

The Hispanic population, designated an ethnicity by the US Census Bureau, is considered autonomously of race, since, as noted in Chapter 1, you can be Black and Hispanic, White and Hispanic, etc. People of Hispanic origin represent 18.2% of the US population.

The impact of recent immigration policy changes, combined with that of COVID, led us to expect a slowing of population growth rates for Hispanics in the United States. This is reflected in the following table and chart.

Population by Ethnicity	2019 Estimates	2024 Projections
Hispanic	59,855,508	60,753,341
Not Hispanic or Latino	269,474,291	278,973,400
Hispanic Population Growth Rates	2000 to 2010	2019 to 2024
Hispanic	43.2%	1.5%
Not Hispanic or Latino	4.9%	3.5%

After increasing by 43.2% from 2000 to 2010, Hispanic population growth will slow to 1.5% by 2024.

Given the large number of Hispanic persons born and raised in the United States, we remain optimistic about prospects for Hispanic businesses, however.

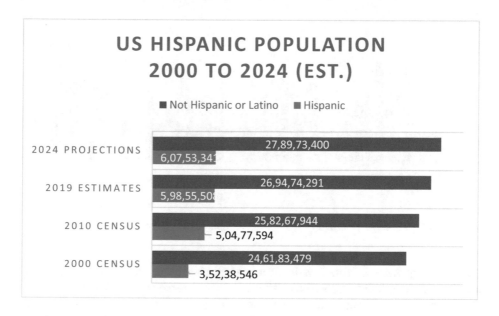

The United States in 2020: Income and Employment

Income

The impact of the crisis on income distribution will be significant. The percentage of households in lower-income categories will grow. Growth in higher-income categories will slow. These factors will lead to a more unequal and extreme income distribution in the United States, with certain implications for minority businesses: understanding these factors will impact product pricing and product strategy. Products that appeal to low-income customers may do better, over time, than those targeted to high-income consumers. This will, of course, depend upon the product offered and the product category.

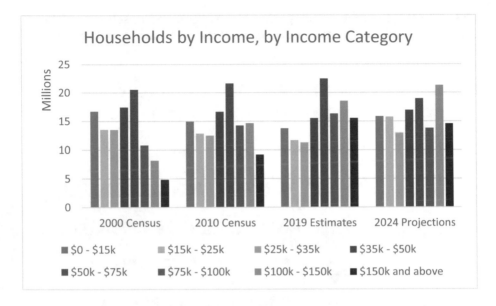

Note the growth in the low-income categories from 2019 to 2024. This implies that products and services that appeal to persons in those groups will have, other things equal, more customers. This, in turn, implies that a luxury strategy, so prevalent in the years leading up to the crisis, may not work post crisis. One of the things the crisis did was focus the attention of the population on the things that really matter – family, food, and life. I suspect that products and services that reflect these changing values will do well.

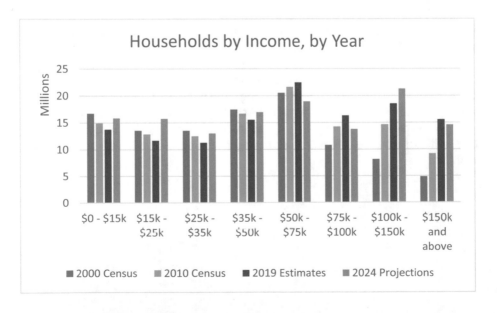

While upper-income households will grow, so will lower-income households. Much of this has to do with specific factors, like immigration; the fact remains that there will be significant opportunity serving lower-income household categories (as Walmart found out).

Households by Income	2019 Estimates	% of Distribution	2024 Projections	% of Distribution
$0 - $15k	13,750,623	11.0%	15,852,720	12.2%
$15k - $25k	11,683,962	9.3%	15,750,149	12.1%
$25k - $35k	11,289,280	9.0%	13,016,652	10.0%
$35k - $50k	15,526,614	12.4%	16,950,545	13.0%
$50k - $75k	22,480,183	18.0%	18,939,229	14.6%
$75k - $100k	16,315,943	13.0%	13,784,634	10.6%
$100k - $150k	18,531,572	14.8%	21,293,941	16.4%
$150k and above	15,542,838	12.4%	14,578,650	11.2%

Households with income from $0 to $50,000 will increase. Having grown drastically in the period from 2000 to 2010, households in higher-income categories are projected to decline from 2019 to 2024.

It's the fact that there are more people in lower-income categories that is important. This means that you cannot count on growth in the number of upper-income groups to support your service or product in the same way that you could in the 1990s or the early 2000s. There will be relatively fewer people in these categories. Of course, your product may be so innovative or focused that these larger trends do not matter. One strategy is to develop products or services that target the growth in lower-income categories, a la Wal-Mart.

Households by Income	Percent Change	
	2000 to 2010	2019 to 2024
$0 - $15k	-10.6%	15.3%
$15k - $25k	-5.0%	34.8%
$25k - $35k	-7.5%	15.3%
$35k - $50k	-4.5%	9.2%
$50k - $75k	5.3%	-15.8%
$75k - $100k	32.0%	-15.5%
$100k - $150k	79.9%	14.9%
$150k and above	90.3%	-6.2%

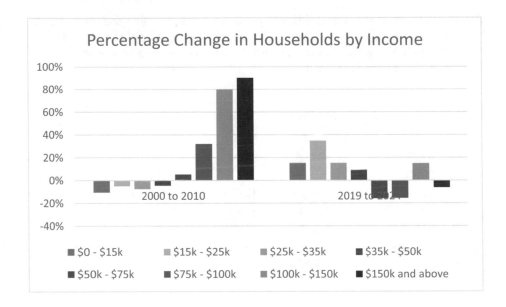

Employment

We estimate COVID employment impacts are severe, of course, given the lockdown and the breadth of the crisis. The number of unemployed persons has increased, as have the number of persons who have left the labor force either on a voluntary or involuntary basis. Blue-collar jobs have grown relative to white-collar jobs.

These facts point to opportunities for minority firms, as we will discuss in later chapters of this book.

	2019 Estimates	2024 Projections
Total Population 16+	263,418,644	274,319,204
Total Labor Force	172,706,267	175,258,451
Civilian, Employed	164,410,008	166,091,835
Civilian, Unemployed	7,183,750	8,627,394
In Armed Forces	1,112,509	1,122,914
Not in Labor Force	90,712,377	107,701,263
% Blue Collar	64,702,048	66,886,777
% White Collar	99,707,960	101,603,608

Unemployment grew dramatically from 2000 to 2010 and is expected to grow from 2019 to 2024. The number of persons not in the labor force will also grow.

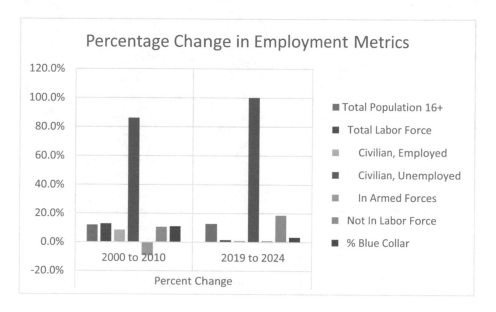

Minority Firms in 2020 and 2021
Impact of COVID-19

According to a recent study,[4] "The number of active business owners in the United States plummeted by 3.3 million or 22 percent over the crucial two-month window from February to April 2020." Minority firms have been especially impacted by COVID-19. African-American businesses experienced a 41 percent drop, while "Latinx business owners fell by 32 percent, and Asian business owners dropped by 26 percent."

---

[4] *The Impact of Covid-19 on Small Business Owners: Evidence of Early-Stage Losses from the April 2020 Current Population Survey.* Robert W. Fairlie. NBER Working Paper No. 27309. June 2020. JEL No. J15,J16,L26.

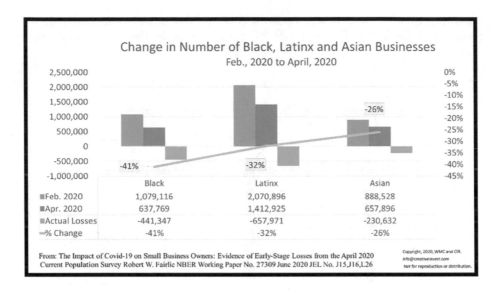

Change in Number of Black, Latinx and Asian Businesses
Feb., 2020 to April, 2020

	Black	Latinx	Asian
■Feb. 2020	1,079,116	2,070,896	888,528
■Apr. 2020	637,769	1,412,925	657,896
■Actual Losses	-441,347	-657,971	-230,632
━% Change	-41%	-32%	-26%

From: The Impact of Covid-19 on Small Business Owners: Evidence of Early-Stage Losses from the April 2020 Current Population Survey Robert W. Fairlie NBER Working Paper No. 27309 June 2020 JEL No. J15,J16,L26

Copyright, 2020, WMC and CIR.
info@creative-invest.com
Not for reproduction or distribution.

As noted by the same study, immigrant business owners suffered a decline of 36%, and female-owned businesses fell by 25%.

An update to this study showed the number of minority firms recovering somewhat.

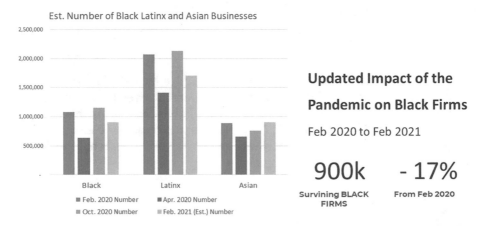

Est. Number of Black Latinx and Asian Businesses

■ Feb. 2020 Number   ■ Apr. 2020 Number
■ Oct. 2020 Number   ■ Feb. 2021 (Est.) Number

Updated Impact of the Pandemic on Black Firms

Feb 2020 to Feb 2021

900k   - 17%

Surivining BLACK FIRMS   From Feb 2020

Source: Fairlie, Robert. 2020. "The Impact of COVID-19 on Small Business Owners: The First Three Months after Social-Distancing Restrictions" Journal of Economics and Management Strategy. (2) Reg. Adjusted estimates are based on regression analysis accounting for trends and seasonality (monthly).

These are serious and significant impacts, the likes of which we have never seen in the modern US economy. Recovering will require an honest look at the situation and a plan. That is what this book is about.

Estimated Industry Impact

Estimates of COVID's impact by industry is available online but

Estimated Change in Number of All Firms by Industry, Feb 2020 to April 2020	Apr-20	Ch in number of firms from Feb 2020	%	Feb-20
Agriculture	928,156	58,494	7%	869,661
Construction	1,768,875	(667,182)	-27%	2,436,057
Manufacturing	506,019	(60,174)	-11%	566,192
Retail Trade	960,872	(107,612)	-10%	1,068,484
Transportation	624,498	(173,827)	-22%	798,325
Financial activities	1,149,105	(152,665)	-12%	1,301,769
Professional and bus	2,695,136	(600,739)	-18%	3,295,875
Health services	1,034,240	(204,094)	-16%	1,238,335
Arts, leisure, hotels	442,964	(242,045)	-35%	685,009
Restaurants	319,194	(90,411)	-22%	409,605
Repair and maintenance	385,400	(127,003)	-25%	512,403
All other industries	895,901	(935,074)	-51%	1,830,976
Nonessential industry	2,292,949	(1,382,990)	-38%	3,675,939
Essential industry	9,417,411	(1,919,342)	-17%	11,336,752

Hotels and leisure establishments declined by 35% from February to April of 2020. Transportation-related firms fell by 22%, no doubt in relation to the decline at hotels. Construction firms fell by 27%.

Demographic Group Losses and Simulations of Business Losses from Switching Industry Distributions Group				
	Feb-20	Apr-20	Losses	% change
Total	15,012,692	11,710,360	-3,302,331	-22%
Female	5,389,399	4,048,205	-1,341,194	-25%
Male	9,623,293	7,662,156	-1,961,137	-20%
Black	1,079,116	637,769	-441,347	-41%
Latinx	2,070,896	1,412,925	-657,971	-32%
Asian	888,528	657,896	-230,632	-26%
White	10,553,415	8,761,531	-1,791,884	-17%
Immigrant	3,120,275	2,009,597	-1,110,677	-36%
Native Born	11,892,417	9,700,763	-2,191,654	-18%

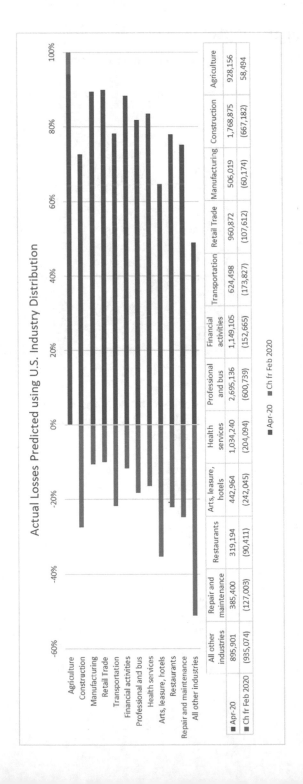

Actual Losses Predicted using U.S. Industry Distribution

	All other industries	Repair and maintenance	Restaurants	Arts, leisure, hotels	Health services	Professional and bus	Financial activities	Transportation	Retail Trade	Manufacturing	Construction	Agriculture
Apr-20	895,901	385,400	319,194	442,964	1,034,240	2,695,136	1,149,105	624,498	960,872	506,019	1,768,875	928,156
Ch fr Feb 2020	(935,074)	(127,003)	(90,411)	(242,045)	(204,094)	(600,739)	(152,665)	(173,827)	(107,612)	(60,174)	(667,182)	58,494

■ Apr-20 ■ Ch fr Feb 2020

Detailed Industry Data, by Ethnic Group

The declines noted earlier are distressing, but they offer the first clue into the way out of the crisis. Many, but not all, of the firms that failed need to be replaced. The decline opens the door for entrants, especially African Americans, to enter industries and professions that may have been difficult to enter prior to the crisis. As with the *Battle of Milliken's Bend*,[5] we anticipate that once given exposure to these new opportunities, minority firms will do well.

To help determine which industries might present opportunities, we need up-to-date information on the current state of minority-owned firms. To obtain, we analyze information from 24 million US businesses and 206 million consumers.

In the data that follows, business activity, ownership information, and minority status are, in general, self-certified. Like Airbnb, Uber, and Lyft, we trust people to honestly report their circumstances. Further, the minority "certification" industry imposes a tax on minority firms, since, in order to receive the (supposed) benefits that come from minority status, individuals seeking certification generally have to pay a third party in order to have their ethnic and/or gender status confirmed. Even in the case of "free" certification programs, like the Federal Government's SBA 8(a) program, program approval requires significant time. We think this is wrong, and will have more to say in later sections of the book.

In the following, we provide August 2020 estimates of the profile and performance of firms.[6]

For our research, we estimate that the number of African American firms in the database totals 80,892. Asian Pacific firms number 25,512. 49,431 Hispanic firms are estimated to exist in the United States. Firms owned by persons from the Indian (Asian) subcontinent are estimated to number 12,319. Native American firms number 11,874. Finally, women-owned firms are represented by two categories: WBE and MWBE. These number 69,636 (minority and women) and 1,067,067 (all women), respectively.

---

[5] The Battle of Milliken's Bend, fought June 7, 1863, was part of the Vicksburg Campaign of the American Civil War. It was distinguished by the prominent role played by the US Colored Troops who, despite lacking much military training, fought bravely with inferior weaponry and defeated a much larger Confederate force.

[6] See notes on the data used and the study assumptions.

Ethnic Group	Number of Firms	Per Firm Revenue Est	Total Estimated Revenue
AfAm	80,892	$ 292,699	$ 23,677,014,788
AsPac	25,512	$ 2,559,624	$ 65,301,126,365
Hispa	49,431	$ 1,073,660	$ 53,072,101,031
Indian-Subc	12,319	$ 1,865,644	$ 22,982,872,435
Nativ	11,874	$ 4,325,338	$ 51,359,068,375
WBE	69,636	$ 365,921	$ 25,481,240,566

AfAM = African American; AsPac = Asian Pacific; Hispa = Hispanic; Indian-Subc = Indian Subcontinent; Nativ – Native American. WBE = Woman Business Enterprise. Source: Gale Business DemographicsNow

This is consistent with historical data. "Minority business" programs began as a response to "government investigation of civil disorder in the nation's inner cities." These investigations "revealed that ... two societies existed—one Black and one White ... separate and unequal." As a result, pressure grew in Congress to use Federal purchasing power to encourage business ownership by African Americans. This, we feel, explains the predominance of African American firms in the data.

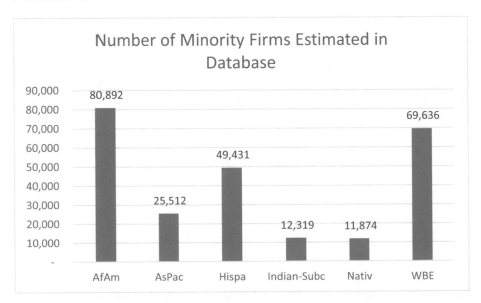

Minority firm revenue estimates are $292,699 for African American firms, $2,559,624 for Asian Pacific firms, $1,073,660 for Hispanic firms, and $1,865,644 for firms owned by persons from the Indian Subcontinent. Native firms are estimated to generate $4.3 million. WBE firms generate $365,000 per year.

We note that these revenue estimates are generally higher than those from other sources. This is a result of the self-certification bias noted before and from the fact that minority businesses from this source tend to be more established firms.

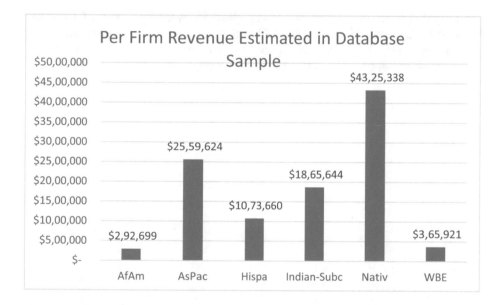

Minority Firms by State

The following tables present color-coded information on the number of minority businesses by state for our sample. Green bars in the following tables represent a higher number of minority firms of that specific ethnic type, at least based on the limited sample of firms we analyzed. Using this data, we both confirm the general accuracy of the sample and reveal states that have a high number of minority business owners of a specific ethnic background. In essence, the tables show the states that are "friendlier" to firms with a certain ethnic ownership type, if, as I assume, more and growing minority firms reflect a more welcoming, supportive environment. I also note the length of the column. This indicates the fact that, for certain firms, geographical location is limited. This may be due to a number of factors, including sample size and historical patterns of settlement and immigration. With a higher number of firms, it is easier to build or join a business community of similarly situated firms. Of course, some may decide or be forced to locate in states where minority business representation is lower.

The following tables show the number of firms owned by African Americans. Georgia leads the list. Texas, Maryland, and Florida establish the top five.

For Asian Pacific firms in the sample, California is the top state. Pennsylvania is second (a result of our small sample), and New York, Florida, Virginia, and Maryland follow.

For Hispanic firms in the sample, Texas leads, followed by Florida, California, New York, Arizona, and Puerto Rico. One thing to note about the sample is the short length of the bar. Immigration policies probably play a role here, since the overall environment may be relatively more hostile to members from this group.

State	AfAm	State	AsianPac	State	Hispa
GA	59	CA	62	TX	116
TX	59	PA	43	FL	105
MD	47	NY	41	CA	69
FL	46	TX	38	NY	27
NY	37	FL	34	AZ	21
CA	30	VA	30	PR	19
VA	28	MD	25	VA	16
IL	19	OH	21	IL	14
OH	19	NC	20	NM	13
PA	18	HI	19	NJ	12
NC	16	WV	17	CO	9
DC	12	KY	16	MD	7
AL	11	GA	13	NC	7
MI	11	IL	11	GA	5
MO	9	TN	11	OR	4
NJ	9	NJ	10	AR	4
SC	9	WA	9	HI	3
LA	8	MA	7	WA	3
AR	5	DE	7	DE	3
IN	5	SC	6	NV	3
OK	5	LA	6	OK	3
AZ	4	IN	6	ID	3
CT	4	AZ	6	PA	2
MA	4	MN	6	OH	2
NV	4	AL	4	TN	2
KY	3	MS	4	MA	2
MS	3	CO	4	SC	2
TN	3	UT	4	LA	2
IA	2	MI	3	MI	2
OR	2	MO	3	MO	2
WA	2	DC	2	DC	2
WI	2	CT	2	CT	2
CO	1	OR	2	KS	2
DE	1	KS	2	NE	2
KS	1	AR	1	WY	2
ME	1	NV	1	KY	1

WV	1	AK	1	IN	1
AK		NE	1	AL	1
HI		NM	1	MS	1
ID		WY	1	UT	1
MN		OK		WI	1
MT		IA		ND	1
ND		WI		WV	
NE		ME		MN	
NH		ID		AK	
NM		MT		IA	
PR		ND		ME	
RI		NH		MT	
SD		PR		NH	
UT		RI		RI	
VT		SD		SD	
WY		VT		VT	

The following tables show the number of firms owned by persons from the Indian Subcontinent. California leads the list, again, consistent with anecdotal evidence. Virginia, Texas, Maryland, and New Jersey round out the top five.

For Native American firms in the sample, Oklahoma leads, followed by Arkansas (perhaps a result of our small sample) and California. Texas, Virginia (sample bias again), and Arizona follow.

One thing to note about the sample of women-owned firms is the broader geographic diversity.

State	IndSub	State	Native	State	Women
CA	85	OK	54	CA	64
VA	66	AK	48	TX	52
TX	50	CA	37	NY	36
MD	45	TX	37	FL	35
NJ	34	VA	31	GA	29
IL	24	AZ	22	VA	19
FL	20	NC	21	MD	19
NY	19	NM	19	IL	17
GA	19	FL	18	NC	16
OH	15	WA	17	CO	12
MI	15	WI	17	NJ	12
MA	10	CO	16	MA	12
IN	9	AL	15	WA	11
PA	8	MN	15	OR	11
LA	8	HI	12	PA	10
NM	7	LA	11	IN	9
WA	7	MD	10	AZ	8
AZ	5	GA	10	SC	8
DC	5	MT	10	MN	7
CO	4	NY	7	LA	7
NC	4	ID	7	ID	7
MO	4	IL	5	TN	7
OR	3	IN	5	OH	7
DE	3	SC	5	CT	7
OK	3	NV	5	MI	6
SC	3	SD	5	MO	6
KY	3	MI	4	IA	6
NV	2	MO	4	OK	5
CT	2	OR	4	WI	5
KS	2	KS	4	NV	5
NE	2	TN	4	NM	4
WY	2	ND	3	HI	4
AL	2	OH	2	MT	4

WV	2	PA	2	DE	4
RI	2	DC	2	KY	3
ID	1	KY	2	NH	3
TN	1	UT	2	AL	2
UT	1	NJ	1	KS	2
MN	1	MA	1	ND	2
NH	1	DE	1	UT	2
PR		CT	1	AR	2
AR		WY	1	NE	2
HI		RI	1	WV	2
MS		AR	1	SD	1
WI		IA	1	DC	1
ND		NE		WY	1
AK		WV		RI	1
IA		NH		PR	1
ME		PR		MS	1
MT		MS		ME	1
SD		ME		VT	1
VT		VT		AK	

The overall picture looks like this:

State	AfAm	State	AsianPac	State	Hispa	State	IndSub	State	Native	State	Women
GA	59	CA	62	TX	116	CA	85	OK	54	CA	64
TX	59	PA	43	FL	105	VA	66	AK	48	TX	52
MD	47	NY	41	CA	69	TX	50	CA	37	NY	36
FL	46	TX	38	AZ	27	MD	45	FL	37	FL	35
NY	37	FL	34	PR	21	NJ	34	VA	31	GA	29
CA	30	VA	30	VA	16	IL	24	AZ	22	VA	19
VA	28	MD	25	IL	14	FL	20	NC	21	MD	19
IL	19	OH	21	NM	13	NY	19	MD	19	IL	17
OH	19	NC	20	GA	12	GA	19	IL	18	NC	16
PA	18	HI	19	OH	9	OH	15	CO	17	CO	12
NC	16	WV	17	MI	7	MI	15	NJ	16	NJ	12
DC	12	KY	16	MA	5	MA	10	MA	15	MA	12
AL	11	GA	13	IN	4	IN	9	WA	15	WA	11
MI	11	IL	11	PA	4	PA	8	OR	15	OR	11
MO	9	TN	11	LA	4	LA	7	PA	12	PA	10
NJ	9	NJ	10	NM	3	NM	7	IN	11	IN	9
SC	9	WA	9	AZ	3	MD	5	AZ	10	AZ	8
LA	8	MA	7	DC	3	GA	5	SC	10	SC	8
AR	5	DE	7	CO	3	MT	5	MN	10	MN	7
IN	5	NV	6	NC	3	NY	4	LA	7	LA	7
OK	5	OK	6	MO	3	ID	4	ID	7	ID	7
AZ	4	ID	6	OR	2	IL	4	TN	5	TN	7
CT	4	AZ	6	DE	2	IN	3	OH	5	OH	7
MA	4	MN	4	OK	2	SC	3	CT	5	CT	7
NV	4	AL	4	SC	2	NV	3	MI	5	MI	6
KY	3	MS	4	KY	2	SD	3	MO	5	MO	6
MS	3	CO	4	NV	2	MI	3	IA	4	IA	6
TN	3	UT	3	CT	2	MO	2	OK	4	OK	5
IA	2	MI	3	KS	2	OR	2	WI	4	WI	5
OR	2	MO	3	NE	2	KS	2	OR	4	NV	5
WA	2	DC	2	WY	2	TN	2	KS	2	NM	4
WI	2	CT	2	KY	1	ND	2	TN	2	HI	4
CO	1	OR	2	IN	1	OH	2	ND	2	MT	4
DE	1	KS	2	AL	1	PA	2	OH	2	DE	4
KS	1	NE	2	MS	1	DC	2	PA	2	KY	3
ME	1	AR	1	UT	1	KY	1	DC	2	NH	3
WV	1	NV	1	WI	1	UT	1	KY	1	AL	2
AK	1	AK	1	ND	1	NJ	1	UT	1	KS	2
HI		NE		WV		MA	1	MA	1	ND	2
ID		NM		MN		DE	1	DE	1	UT	2
MN		WY		UT	1	CT		AR	1	AR	2
MT		OK		WI		WY		NE	1	NE	2
ND		IA		ND		RI		WV	1	WV	2
NE		WI		WV		HI		RI		SD	1
NH		ME		MN		MS		IA		DC	1
NM		ID		AK		WI		NE		WY	
PR		MT		IA		ND		WV		RI	
RI		ND		ME		IA		PR		PR	
SD		NH		MT		ME		MS		MS	
UT		PR		NH		MT		ME		ME	
VT		RI		RI		SD		VT		VT	
WY		SD		SD		VT		AK		AK	

Minority Firms by Occupation/Industry

The following tables present color-coded information on the number of minority businesses by occupation, as defined by eight-digit SIC codes. They have been truncated to show the top results, as the full tables run to 800 rows. As before, green bars in the following tables represent a higher number of minority firms of that specific ethnic type in that specific occupation, again based on the limited sample of firms we analyzed.

The data in general confirm our thinking about the general accuracy of the sample and show us which occupations have a high number of minority business owners of a specific ethnic background. In essence, the tables show occupations that may be "friendlier" to business owners with a certain ethnic background. As before, the length of the column is significant. This indicates the fact that, for certain minority groups, occupational opportunities remain limited. As with the geographical analysis, there is much to be said for starting a business in an occupation with limited minority representation.

Summary: The number one industry in our sample data for African American businesses is Business Services not elsewhere classified, no specific kind. This is a catch-all category that includes businesses "such as bondspersons, drafting services, lecture bureaus, notaries public, sign painting, speakers' bureaus, water softening services, and auctioneering services, on a commission or fee basis."

One reason why this category is so prevalent is its breadth. It includes

Agents and brokers for authors and nonperforming artist	Metal slitting and shearing on a contract or fee basis
Apparel pressing service for the trade	Meter readers, remote
Appraisers, except real estate appraisers	Microfilm recording and developing service
Arbitration and conciliation services	Mounting merchandise on cards on a contract or fee basis
Artists' agents and brokers, except performing artists	Music distribution systems, except coin-operated
Auctioneering service on a commission or fee basis	Notaries public
Authors' agents and brokers	Packaging and labeling service (not packing and crating)
Automobile recovery service	Paralegal service
Automobile repossession service	Parcel packing service (packaging)
Automobile shows, flower shows, and home shows: promoters of	Patent brokers
Bartering services for businesses	Patrol of electric transmission or gas lines
Batik work (handprinting on textiles)	Photogrammetric mapping service (not professional engineers)
Bondspersons	Photographic library service, still
Bottle exchanges	Photography brokers
Bronzing baby shoes	Pipeline and power line inspection services
Business brokers (buying and selling business enterprises)	Playwrights' brokers
Charge account service (shopping plates) collection by individual	Post office contract stations
Check validation service	Presorting mail service
Cloth: cutting to length, bolting, or winding for textile distributors	Press clipping service
Contractors' disbursement control	Printed circuitry graphic layout
Convention bureaus	Process serving service
Convention decorators	Produce weighing service, not connected with transportation
Copyright protection service	Product sterilization service
Correct time service	Promoters of home shows and flower shows
Cosmetic kits, assembling and packaging	Racetrack cleaning, except buildings
Cotton inspection service, not connected with transportation	Radio broadcasting music checkers
Cotton sampler service	Radio transcription service
Coupon redemption service, except trading stamps	Recording studios on a contract or fee basis
Credit card service (collection by individual firms)	Redemption of trading stamps
Decoration service for special events	Repossession service
Demonstration service, separate from sale	Restaurant reservation service
Directories, telephone: distribution on a contract or fee basis	Rug binding for the trade
Divers, commercial	Safety inspection service, except automotive
Drafting service, except temporary help	Salvaging of damaged merchandise, not engaged in sales
Drawback service, customs	Sampling of commodities, not connected with transportation
Drive-a-way automobile service	Scrap steel cutting on a contract or fee basis
Embroidering of advertising on shirts, etc.	Shoe designers
Engrossing, e.g., diplomas and resolutions	Showcard painting
Exhibits, building of: by industrial contractors	Shrinking textiles for tailors and dressmakers
Field warehousing, not public warehousing	Sign painting and lettering shops
Filling pressure containers (aerosol) with hair spray, insecticides, etc.	Solvents recovery service on a contract or fee basis
Fire extinguishers, service of	Speakers' bureaus
Firefighting service, other than forestry or public	Sponging textiles for tailors and dressmakers
Flagging service (traffic control)	Styling of fashions, apparel, furniture, and textiles
Floats, decoration of	Styling wigs for the trade
Florists' telegraph service	Swimming pool cleaning and maintenance
Folding and refolding service: textile and apparel	Switchboard operation of private branch exchanges
Fundraising on a contract or fee basis	Tape slitting for the trade (cutting plastics, leather, etc. into widths)
Gas systems, contract conversion from manufactured to natural gas	Tax collection agencies: collecting for a city, county, or State
Handtool designers	Tax title dealers: agencies for city, county, or State
Handwriting analysis	Telemarketing (telephone marketing) service on a contract or fee basis
Hosiery pairing on a contract or fee basis	Telephone answering, except beeper service
Hotel reservation service	Telephone solicitation service on a contract or fee basis
Identification engraving service	Textile designers
Inspection of commodities, not connected with transportation	Textile folding and packing services
Interior decorating consulting service, except painters and paper	Time-share condominium exchanges
Interior designing service, except painters and paper hangers	Tobacco sheeting service on a contract or fee basis
Inventory computing service	Tourist information bureaus
Labeling bottles, cans, cartons, etc. for the trade: not printing	Trade show arrangement
Laminating of photographs (coating photographs with plastics)	Trading stamp promotion and sale to stores
Lecture bureaus	Trading stamp redemption
Lettering service	Translation service
Liquidators of merchandise on a contract or fee basis	Water softener service
Mannequin decorating service	Weighing foods and other commodities not connected with
Map drafting service	Welcoming service
Mapmaking, including aerial	Window trimming service
Message service, telephone answering except beeper service	Yacht brokers

Other top occupations include transportation services, trucking, real estate, and building maintenance (as noted, the following table is limited to the top occupations; see the book's page on www.apress.com for details on how to download the entire table).

Business Description	AfAm
Business services, NEC, NSK	76
Management consulting services	27
Business consulting, NEC, nsk	25
Transportation services, NEC, nsk	21
Local trucking, without storage, nsk	17
Real estate agents and managers	17
Building maintenance services, NEC, nsk	12
Management services, nsk	12
Trucking, except local	11
Custom computer programming services, nsk	10
Repair services, NEC, nsk	10
Single-family housing construction, nsk	10

SUMMARY: As with our sample data for African American businesses, the number one industry for Asian Pacific businesses is Business Services not elsewhere classified, no specific kind.

Other top industries and occupations include business consulting and computer programming services.

Business Description2	AsianPac
Business services, NEC, nsk	19
Business consulting, NEC, nsk	13
Custom computer programming services, nsk	12
Hotels and motels, nsk	12
Engineering services, nsk	10
Management services, nsk	5
Electrical work, nsk	5
Nonresidential building operators	5
Top and body repair and paint shops	5
Nondurable goods, NEC, nsk	5

SUMMARY: For Hispanic-owned businesses, single-family home construction, building maintenance, electrical work, and special trade contractors are also top industries.

Business Description3	Hispa
Business services, NEC, nsk	43
Single-family housing construction, nsk	19
Real estate agents and managers	17
Plumbing, heating, air-conditioning, nsk	15
Custom computer programming services, nsk	14
Business consulting, NEC, nsk	13
Building maintenance services, NEC, nsk	13
Electrical work, nsk	12
Management consulting services	12
Engineering services, nsk	10

The following data confirms our perceptions about firms owned by persons from the Indian Subcontinent. Computer programming services are the top occupation. Other top occupations and industries include hotels and motels, again, confirming anecdotal information.

Business Description4	IndSub
Custom computer programming services, nsk	59
Business consulting, NEC, nsk	38
Computer related services, NEC, nsk	36
Business services, NEC, nsk	29
Hotels and motels, nsk	21
Engineering services, nsk	20
Management consulting services	15
Computer integrated systems design, nsk	14
Nonresidential construction, NEC, nsk	13
Offices and clinics medical doctors,nsk	11
Commercial physical research, nsk	11

For Native Americans, the legacy of severe discrimination limits business opportunity, as shown in the following summary table. The categories shown all fall into the most general of business activities, without the specialization of, say, persons from the Indian Subcontinent.

Business Description5	Native
Business services, NEC, nsk	29
Nonresidential construction, NEC, nsk	24
Business consulting, NEC, nsk	23
Engineering services, nsk	15
Management consulting services	15
Single-family housing construction, nsk	11
Facilities support services	11
Industrial buildings and warehouses	11
Management services, nsk	10
Plumbing, heating, air-conditioning, nsk	9

As with Native Americans, the legacy of gender discrimination is clearly evident in the summary table of occupational categories from women-owned firms. Note the addition of beauty shops and child care services.

Business Description6	Women
Business services, NEC, nsk	46
Beauty shops	28
Real estate agents and managers	22
Child day care services, nsk	16
Business consulting, NEC, nsk	13
Management consulting services	13
Repair services, NEC, nsk	12
Eating places	12
Grocery stores, nsk	11
Employment agencies, nsk	10

The graph shows the number of occupations in the data sample:

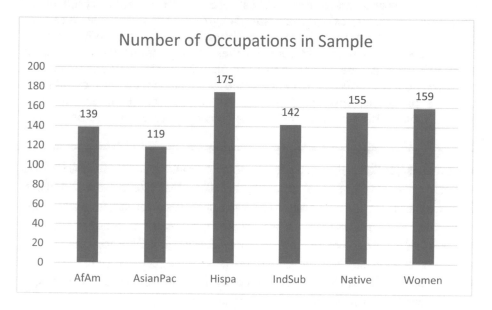

A higher number of industries and occupations points to more resiliency: one of the keys to surviving is having a number of things you can do, to increase the number of jobs you can take.

Competition from Other Groups

While the preceding data provides insight into the current state of minority businesses, one issue for African American and other minority firms is the competition from other groups. When business programs for African American businesses were established, almost immediately, program managers moved to expand the definition of "minority," most notably with the addition of white women to the mix.[7] These extended definitions are the dominant feature of minority business programs today.

---

[7] In point of fact, the primary economic beneficiaries of the civil rights movement of the 1960s have been white women. According to the US Labor Department, the primary beneficiaries of affirmative action are white women. The Department of Labor estimated that six million white women workers are in higher occupational classifications today than they would have been without affirmative action policies.

As resources for minority business programs increased, other, formerly nonminority groups started to establish programs that would result in the allocation of resources to their specific group. These include "veteran's programs" and programs dedicated to "labor surplus" areas. While there is some overlap in membership between these groups (minority veterans, for example), there can be no doubt that the main impact of these programs has been to siphon resources away from the original beneficiaries of minority business programs, specifically African Americans, to members of other groups. Competition *between* minority groups has also been a factor.

■ **What's Going on Here**   Hypercompetition refers to the negative effects of an unbridled fight for resources that uses the "free market" philosophy unleashed in the 1980s as justification for a set of policies that elevate money over human community. Under this set of attitudes, market power, money, and celebrity are worshipped, to the exclusion of cooperation in support of community. Most policy makers and economists are overly concerned with hyperinflation, the runaway decline in the value of a currency. Hypercompetition, in fact, has, at its apex, a much more damaging impact on the fabric of society, not just its money. New monetary technologies, including digital currencies like Bitcoin, may limit the impact of hyperinflation.

This has led to a lower allocation of resources to African Americans, the original intended recipients of minority business development programs. (We will discuss original program goals in the next chapter.)

Selected Laws, Programs, and Regulations

A Few of the Laws and Regulations Designed to Support Minority Businesses

This chapter contains summary information on selected US laws that assist minority-owned businesses, including details on the Offices of Minority and Women Inclusion (OMWI) from Dodd-Frank. Section 342 of the Dodd-Frank Wall Street Reform and Consumer Protection Act contains a "provision creating an Office of Minority and Women Inclusion at various agencies to monitor the diversity efforts of the agencies, the regulated entities and agency contractors."

"Minority business" programs began as a response to civil disorder in the nation's cities. Government investigations "revealed that … two societies existed—one Black and one White … separate and unequal."

© William Michael Cunningham 2021
W. M. Cunningham, *Thriving As a Minority-Owned Business in Corporate America*,
https://doi.org/10.1007/978-1-4842-7240-4_3

In an effort to correct this situation, several laws were proposed, and minority business programs created. Unfortunately, these issues persist and contributed to the extreme impact COVID had on minority communities.

Still, it is our belief that being aware of laws in place in this area would be beneficial to readers of this book. If you are going to try to use resources provided by these laws, you should probably know, exactly, what they say.

At the end of the chapter, we provide suggestions on using these resources.

■ **Note**   This is not a comprehensive review of laws and regulations in this sector, nor is it meant to be "legal advice." Consult an attorney if you need information or advice relevant to your specific situation; also note that there are many national, state, and local organizations focused on minority business development.

This chapter will also highlight unused and unrecognized resources at the federal level.

We do so in order to enable you to understand where federal minority business programs started and where they are now.

History of Federal Minority Business Laws

In 1942, the Smaller War Plants Corporation (SWPC) was the first US entity that "authorized a federal agency to enter into prime contracts with other agencies and subcontract with small businesses." Unfortunately, SWPC's "authority expired, along with the SWPC, at the end of the World War II." These small business efforts were not specifically focused or directed toward minority firms, however.

The next federal agency created for the purpose of supporting small businesses was the Small Defense Plants Administration (SDPA), created in 1951. SDPA was created with the same goals that SWPC had. In 1953, SDPA's subcontracting authority was transferred to the Small Business Administration (SBA). According to the GAO

> When the Small Business Act of 1958 transformed the SBA into a permanent agency, this subcontracting authority was included in Section 8(a) of the act.

We believe federal programs for racial and ethnic minorities began on June 25, 1941, with Franklin Delano Roosevelt's Executive Order requiring that all federal agencies include a clause in defense-related contracts prohibiting contractors from discriminating on the basis of "race, creed, color, or national origin." The Order, reproduced as follows, focused on employment, however, not entrepreneurship.

■ FDR's Executive Order 8802   Reaffirming Policy of Full Participation in The Defense Program by All Persons, regardless of Race, Creed, Color, Or National Origin, And Directing Certain Action in Furtherance of Said Policy

June 25, 1941

WHEREAS it is the policy of the United States to encourage full participation in the national defense program by all citizens of the United States, regardless of race, creed, color, or national origin, in the firm belief that the democratic way of life within the Nation can be defended successfully only with the help and support of all groups within its borders; and

WHEREAS there is evidence that available and needed workers have been barred from employment in industries engaged in defense production solely because of consideration of race, creed, color, or national origin, to the detriment of workers' morale and of national unity:

NOW, THEREFORE, by virtue of the authority vested in me by the Constitution and the statutes, and as a prerequisite to the successful conduct of our national defense production effort, I do hereby reaffirm the policy of the United States that there shall be no discrimination in the employment of workers in defense industries or government because of race, creed, color, or national origin, and I do hereby declare that it is the duty of employers and of labor organizations, in furtherance of said policy and of this Order, to provide for the full and equitable participation of all workers in defense industries, without discrimination because of race, creed, color, or national origin;

And it is hereby ordered as follows:

1. All departments and agencies of the Government of the United States concerned with vocational and training programs for defense production shall take special measures appropriate to assure that such programs are administered without discrimination because of race, creed, color, or national origin;

2. All contracting agencies of the Government of the United States shall include in all defense contracts hereafter negotiated by them a provision obligating the contractor not to discriminate against any worker because of race, creed, color, or national origin;

3. There is established in the Office of Production Management a Committee on Fair Employment Practice, which shall consist of a Chairman and four other members to be appointed by the President. The Chairman and members of the Committee shall serve as such without compensation but shall be entitled to actual and necessary transportation, subsistence, and other expenses incidental to performance of their duties. The Committee shall receive and investigate complaints of discrimination in violation of the provisions of this Order and shall take appropriate steps to redress grievances which it finds to be valid. The Committee shall

also recommend to the several departments and agencies of the Government of the United States and to the President all measures which may be deemed by it necessary or proper to effectuate the provisions of this Order.

Franklin D. Roosevelt

The White House

The following are additional minority business–focused Executive Orders issued by various presidents over the years:

Executive Order No. 8802, "Reaffirming Policy of Full Participation in the Defense Program by All Persons, Regardless of Race, Creed, Color, or National Origin, and Directing Certain Action in Furtherance of Said Policy," 6 Federal Register 3109, June 25, 1941.

Executive Order No. 9346, "Further Amending Executive Order No. 8802 by Establishing a New Committee on Fair Employment Practice and Defining its Powers and Duties," 8 Federal Register 7182, May 29, 1943.

Executive Order No. 10308, "Improving the Means for Obtaining Compliance With the Nondiscrimination Provisions of Federal Contracts," 16 Federal Register 12303, December 3, 1951 (Truman).

Executive Order No. 10557, "Approving the Revised Provision in Government Contracts Relating to Nondiscrimination in Employment," 19 Federal Register 5655, September 3, 1954 (Eisenhower).

Executive Order No. 10925, "Establishing the President's Committee on Equal Employment Opportunity," 26 Federal Register 1977, March 6, 1961 (Kennedy).

Executive Order No. 11458, "Prescribing Arrangements for Developing and Coordinating a National Program for Minority Business Enterprise," 34 Federal Register 4937, March 7, 1969 (Nixon).

The National Advisory Commission on Civil Disorders (known as the Kerner Commission after its chair, Governor Otto Kerner, Jr. of Illinois), Report of the National Advisory Commission on Civil Disorders (U.S. GPO, 1968), p. 21.

Executive Order No. 11625, "Prescribing Additional Arrangements for Developing and Coordinating a National Program for Minority Business Enterprise," 36 Federal Register 19967, October 13, 1971. (Nixon).

Executive Order On Advancing Racial Equity and Support for Underserved Communities Through the Federal Government. January 20, 2021. (Biden).

■ **Executive Order On Advancing Racial Equity and Support for Underserved Communities Through the Federal Government**

JANUARY 20, 2021 • PRESIDENTIAL ACTIONS

By the authority vested in me as President by the Constitution and the laws of the United States of America, it is hereby ordered:

Section 1. Policy. Equal opportunity is the bedrock of American democracy, and our diversity is one of our country's greatest strengths. But for too many, the American Dream remains out of reach. Entrenched disparities in our laws and public policies, and in our public and private institutions, have often denied that equal opportunity to individuals and communities. Our country faces converging economic, health, and climate crises that have exposed and exacerbated inequities, while a historic movement for justice has highlighted the unbearable human costs of systemic racism. Our Nation deserves an ambitious whole-of-government equity agenda that matches the scale of the opportunities and challenges that we face.

It is therefore the policy of my Administration that the Federal Government should pursue a comprehensive approach to advancing equity for all, including people of color and others who have been historically underserved, marginalized, and adversely affected by persistent poverty and inequality. Affirmatively advancing equity, civil rights, racial justice, and equal opportunity is the responsibility of the whole of our Government. Because advancing equity requires a systematic approach to embedding fairness in decision-making processes, executive departments and agencies (agencies) must recognize and work to redress inequities in their policies and programs that serve as barriers to equal opportunity.

By advancing equity across the Federal Government, we can create opportunities for the improvement of communities that have been historically underserved, which benefits everyone. For example, an analysis shows that closing racial gaps in wages, housing credit, lending opportunities, and access to higher education would amount to an additional $5 trillion in gross domestic product in the American economy over the next 5 years. The Federal Government's goal in advancing equity is to provide everyone with the opportunity to reach their full potential. Consistent with these aims, each agency must assess whether, and to what extent, its programs and policies perpetuate systemic barriers to opportunities and benefits for people of color and other underserved groups. Such assessments will better equip agencies to develop policies and programs that deliver resources and benefits equitably to all.

Sec. 2. Definitions. For purposes of this order: (a) The term "equity" means the consistent and systematic fair, just, and impartial treatment of all individuals, including individuals who belong to underserved communities that have been denied such treatment, such as Black, Latino, and Indigenous and Native American persons, Asian Americans and Pacific Islanders and other persons of color; members of religious minorities; lesbian, gay, bisexual, transgender, and queer (LG-BTQ+) persons; persons with disabilities; persons who live in rural areas; and persons otherwise adversely affected by persistent poverty or inequality.

(b) The term "underserved communities" refers to populations sharing a particular characteristic, as well as geographic communities, that have been systematically denied a full opportunity to participate in aspects of economic, social, and civic life, as exemplified by the list in the preceding definition of "equity."

Sec. 3. Role of the Domestic Policy Council. The role of the White House Domestic Policy Council (DPC) is to coordinate the formulation and implementation of my Administration's domestic policy objectives. Consistent with this role, the DPC will coordinate efforts to embed equity principles, policies, and approaches across the Federal Government. This will include efforts to remove systemic barriers to and provide equal access to opportunities and benefits, identify communities the Federal Government has underserved, and develop policies designed to advance equity for those communities. The DPC-led interagency process will ensure that these efforts are made in coordination with the directors of the National Security Council and the National Economic Council.

Sec. 4. Identifying Methods to Assess Equity. (a) The Director of the Office of Management and Budget (OMB) shall, in partnership with the heads of agencies, study methods for assessing whether agency policies and actions create or exacerbate barriers to full and equal participation by all eligible individuals. The study should aim to identify the best methods, consistent with applicable law, to assist agencies in assessing equity with respect to race, ethnicity, religion, income, geography, gender identity, sexual orientation, and disability.

(b) As part of this study, the Director of OMB shall consider whether to recommend that agencies employ pilot programs to test model assessment tools and assist agencies in doing so.

(c) Within 6 months of the date of this order, the Director of OMB shall deliver a report to the President describing the best practices identified by the study and, as appropriate, recommending approaches to expand use of those methods across the Federal Government.

Sec. 5. Conducting an Equity Assessment in Federal Agencies. The head of each agency, or designee, shall, in consultation with the Director of OMB, select certain of the agency's programs and policies for a review that will assess whether underserved communities and their members face systemic barriers in accessing benefits and opportunities available pursuant to those policies and programs. The head of each agency, or designee, shall conduct such review and within 200 days of the date of this order provide a report to the Assistant to the President for Domestic Policy (APDP) reflecting findings on the following:

(a) Potential barriers that underserved communities and individuals may face to enrollment in and access to benefits and services in Federal programs;

(b) Potential barriers that underserved communities and individuals may face in taking advantage of agency procurement and contracting opportunities;

(c) Whether new policies, regulations, or guidance documents may be necessary to advance equity in agency actions and programs; and

(d) The operational status and level of institutional resources available to offices or divisions within the agency that are responsible for advancing civil rights or whose mandates specifically include serving underrepresented or disadvantaged communities.

Sec. 6. Allocating Federal Resources to Advance Fairness and Opportunity. The Federal Government should, consistent with applicable law, allocate resources to address the historic failure to invest sufficiently, justly, and equally in underserved communities, as well as individuals from those communities. To this end:

(a) The Director of OMB shall identify opportunities to promote equity in the budget that the President submits to the Congress.

(b) The Director of OMB shall, in coordination with the heads of agencies, study strategies, consistent with applicable law, for allocating Federal resources in a manner that increases investment in underserved communities, as well as individuals from those communities. The Director of OMB shall report the findings of this study to the President.

Sec. 7. Promoting Equitable Delivery of Government Benefits and Equitable Opportunities. Government programs are designed to serve all eligible individuals. And Government contracting and procurement opportunities should be available on an equal basis to all eligible providers of goods and services. To meet these objectives and to enhance compliance with existing civil rights laws:

(a) Within 1 year of the date of this order, the head of each agency shall consult with the APDP and the Director of OMB to produce a plan for addressing:

　(i) any barriers to full and equal participation in programs identified pursuant to section 5(a) of this order; and

　(ii) any barriers to full and equal participation in agency procurement and contracting opportunities identified pursuant to section 5(b) of this order.

(b) The Administrator of the U.S. Digital Service, the United States Chief Technology Officer, the Chief Information Officer of the United States, and the heads of other agencies, or their designees, shall take necessary actions, consistent with applicable law, to support agencies in developing such plans.

Sec. 8. Engagement with Members of Underserved Communities. In carrying out this order, agencies shall consult with members of communities that have been historically underrepresented in the Federal Government and underserved by, or subject to discrimination in, Federal policies and programs. The head of each agency shall evaluate opportunities, consistent with applicable law, to increase coordination, communication, and engagement with community-based organizations and civil rights organizations.

Sec. 9. Establishing an Equitable Data Working Group. Many Federal datasets are not disaggregated by race, ethnicity, gender, disability, income, veteran status, or other key demographic variables. This lack of data has cascading effects and impedes efforts to measure and advance equity. A first step to promoting equity in Government action is to gather the data necessary to inform that effort.

(a) Establishment. There is hereby established an Interagency Working Group on Equitable Data (Data Working Group).

(b) Membership.

   (i) The Chief Statistician of the United States and the United States Chief Technology Officer shall serve as Co-Chairs of the Data Working Group and coordinate its work. The Data Working Group shall include representatives of agencies as determined by the Co-Chairs to be necessary to complete the work of the Data Working Group, but at a minimum shall include the following officials, or their designees:

   (A) the Director of OMB;

   (B) the Secretary of Commerce, through the Director of the U.S. Census Bureau;

   (C) the Chair of the Council of Economic Advisers;

   (D) the Chief Information Officer of the United States;

   (E) the Secretary of the Treasury, through the Assistant Secretary of the Treasury for Tax Policy;

   (F) the Chief Data Scientist of the United States; and

   (G) the Administrator of the U.S. Digital Service.

   (ii) The DPC shall work closely with the Co-Chairs of the Data Working Group and assist in the Data Working Group's interagency coordination functions.

   (iii) The Data Working Group shall consult with agencies to facilitate the sharing of information and best practices, consistent with applicable law.

(c) Functions. The Data Working Group shall:

    (i) through consultation with agencies, study and provide recommendations to the APDP identifying inadequacies in existing Federal data collection programs, policies, and infrastructure across agencies, and strategies for addressing any deficiencies identified; and

    (ii) support agencies in implementing actions, consistent with applicable law and privacy interests, that expand and refine the data available to the Federal Government to measure equity and capture the diversity of the American people.

(d) OMB shall provide administrative support for the Data Working Group, consistent with applicable law.

Sec. 10. Revocation. (a) Executive Order 13950 of September 22, 2020 (Combating Race and Sex Stereotyping), is hereby revoked.

(b) The heads of agencies covered by Executive Order 13950 shall review and identify proposed and existing agency actions related to or arising from Executive Order 13950. The head of each agency shall, within 60 days of the date of this order, consider suspending, revising, or rescinding any such actions, including all agency actions to terminate or restrict contracts or grants pursuant to Executive Order 13950, as appropriate and consistent with applicable law.

(c) Executive Order 13958 of November 2, 2020 (Establishing the President's Advisory 1776 Commission), is hereby revoked.

Sec. 11. General Provisions. (a) Nothing in this order shall be construed to impair or otherwise affect:

(i) the authority granted by law to an executive department or agency, or the head thereof; or

(ii) the functions of the Director of the Office of Management and Budget relating to budgetary, administrative, or legislative proposals.

(b) This order shall be implemented consistent with applicable law and subject to the availability of appropriations.

(c) Independent agencies are strongly encouraged to comply with the provisions of this order.

(d) This order is not intended to, and does not, create any right or benefit, substantive or procedural, enforceable at law or in equity by any party against the United States, its departments, agencies, or entities, its officers, employees, or agents, or any other person.

JOSEPH R. BIDEN JR.

THE WHITE HOUSE,

January 20, 2021.

By requiring a comprehensive review, the Biden Administration hopes to get to the bottom of the blockages and impediments that impact so many minorities and the firms they create. This level of scrutiny is unprecedented.

As a statement of intended policy, this executive order is helpful in marking the Administration's broad-based perspective on these issues, their intended support for minority businesses, and the direction in which they intend to proceed. The order lacks the full power of law: as noted, it does not "create any right or benefit, substantive or procedural, enforceable at law or in equity by any party against the United States."

This means it cannot be used in a Court of Law to claim, well, anything. It is, however, a welcome change from the prior Administration.

■ **Note** FDR's Executive Order 8802 was very forward looking. It reestablished the intention of the United States Government to treat all of its citizens with respect, to help them achieve "the American Dream." Clearly, progress has been slow. The most recent Executive Order that comes close to the spirit of FDR's is the order issued by the Biden Administration on January 20, 2021. That's a delay of 79 years, 6 months, 26 days.

Disparity Studies

A series of lawsuits established the requirement that minority business advocates prove minority businesses were being discriminated against before public (and private) entities could create and implement programs to redress discrimination by providing monetary benefits to these firms. This research is known as a "disparity study" and makes it much more difficult to provide assistance to firms based on the ethnic and gender makeup of their ownership. This, in turn, limits the ability of minority firms to get ahead, which was the goal of the requirement.

The key legal cases were City of Richmond v. J.A. Croson Co. (488 US 469 (1989)) and Adarand Constructors Inc. v. Peña (515 US 200 (1995)). Of course, given recent evidence, we believe the assumption of discrimination should go unchallenged and that entities should be required to prove that they do not discriminate before any legal challenge to minority business programs is accepted.

To add insult to injury, a cottage industry has grown up of mainly white and non-African American firms that derive significant economic advantage by conducting these studies.

These studies are, for the most part, unnecessary, as the graphic in Figure 3-1 suggests.

Name	Date of Incident	City, State
Emmett Till	8/28/1955	Money, Mississippi
Clifford Glover	4/28/1973	New York City, New York
Amadou Diallo	2/4/1999	New York City, New York
Sean Bell	11/25/2006	Queens, New York
Oscar Grant	1/1/2009	Oakland, California
Aiyana Jones	5/16/2010	Detroit, Michigan
Trayvon Martin	2/26/2012	Sanford, Florida
Jordan Davis	11/23/2012	Jacksonville, Florida
Jonathan Ferrell	9/14/2013	Charlotte, North Carolina
Renisha McBride	11/2/2013	Dearborn Heights, Michigan
Eric Garner	7/17/2014	Staten Island, New York
John Crawford III	8/5/2014	Beavercreek, Ohio
Michael Brown Jr.	8/9/2014	Ferguson, Missouri
Tamir Rice	11/22/2014	Cleveland, Ohio
Anthony Hill	3/9/2015	Chamblee, Georgia
Walter Scott	4/4/2015	North Charleston, South Carolina
Freddie Gray	4/12/2015	Baltimore, Maryland
Tywanza Sanders	6/17/2015	Charleston, South Carolina
Susie Jackson	6/17/2015	Charleston, South Carolina
Rev. Clementa Pinckney	6/17/2015	Charleston, South Carolina
Ethel Lee Lance	6/17/2015	Charleston, South Carolina
Rev. Depayne Middleton-Doctor	6/17/2015	Charleston, South Carolina
Rev. Daniel L. Simmons	6/17/2015	Charleston, South Carolina
Cynthia Hurd	6/17/2015	Charleston, South Carolina
Rev. Sharonda Coleman-Singleton	6/17/2015	Charleston, South Carolina
Myra Thompson	6/17/2015	Charleston, South Carolina
Sandra Bland	7/13/2015	Hempstead, Texas
Samuel DuBose	7/19/2015	Cincinnati, Ohio
Corey Jones	10/18/2015	Palm Beach Gardens, Florida
Alton Sterling	7/5/2016	Baton Rouge, Louisiana
Terence Crutcher	9/16/2016	Tulsa, Oklahoma
Keith Lamont Scott	9/20/2016	Charlotte, North Carolina
Stephon Clark	3/18/2018	Sacramento, California
Botham Jean	9/6/2018	Dallas, Texas
Atatiana Jefferson	10/12/2019	Fort Worth, Texas
Ahmaud Arbery	2/23/2020	Glynn County, Georgia

Figure 3-1. Our Disparity Study

The SBA 8(a) Program

According to the US Government Accountability Office (GAO), the US Small Business Administration's (SBA) "Minority Small Business and Capital Ownership Development Program"—commonly known as the '8(a) Program'—provides participating small businesses with training, technical assistance, and contracting opportunities in the form of **set-aside** and **sole-source** awards.

A **set-aside** contract is one for which only minority contractors may compete. A **sole-source** contract award is one granted without competition. In 1978, Congress gave the SBA explicit authority for the 8(a) Program's mandate that the SBA "can only subcontract with 'socially and economically disadvantaged small business concerns,' or businesses that are least 51% owned by one or more socially and economically disadvantaged individuals and whose management and daily operations are controlled by such individual(s)."

■ **Socially Disadvantaged Individuals are** those who have been "subjected to racial or ethnic prejudice or cultural bias because of their identity as a member of a group without regard to their individual qua**lities."**

■ **Economically Disadvantaged Individuals are defined as** "those socially disadvantaged individuals whose ability to compete in the free enterprise system has been impaired due to diminished capital and credit opportunities as compared to others in the same business area who are not socially disadva**ntaged."**

Both definitions were established so as to include disadvantaged whites.

As the following chart shows, the 8(a) Program awarded $30 billion in contracts to minority firms in FY 2019. While this is a large number, less than 1% of minority firms were helped by the program, and as a percentage of all Federal contracts, the dollar amount going to minority firms, at 5% in FY 2019, fails to reflect the growing importance and significance of minority firms in the United States.

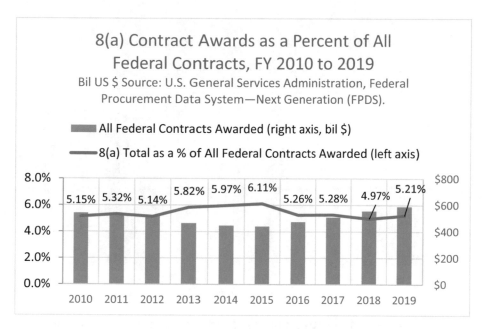

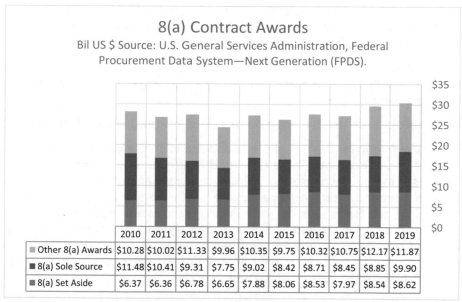

	2010	2011	2012	2013	2014	2015	2016	2017	2018	2019
■ Other 8(a) Awards	$10.28	$10.02	$11.33	$9.96	$10.35	$9.75	$10.32	$10.75	$12.17	$11.87
■ 8(a) Sole Source	$11.48	$10.41	$9.31	$7.75	$9.02	$8.42	$8.71	$8.45	$8.85	$9.90
■ 8(a) Set Aside	$6.37	$6.36	$6.78	$6.65	$7.88	$8.06	$8.53	$7.97	$8.54	$8.62

As you can also see from the following chart, relative to the total number of minority firms in the United States, the number of 8(a) contracts going to those firms is very small; thus, as an effective business development tool, this program is limited. We would need to see a breakout of this data by race and would need to see contracts going to at least 100,000 firms to have an actual impact.

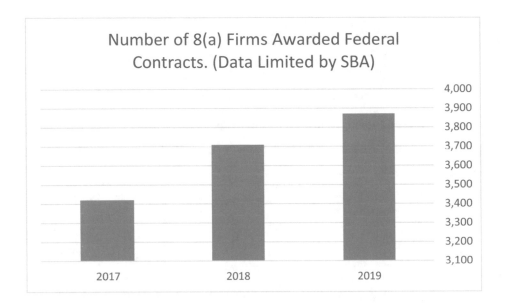

The 8(a) program is effective only for a very small portion of all minority firms: as a percentage of the estimated total number of minority firms, only 0.35% receive an actual Federal government contract from this source. This means that for 99.7% of minority firms, this source is unavailable.

For Black firms, the picture is even more damaging. As we have noted, many of the minority firms receiving benefits are non-Black, non-native African American minority firms.

Those that can use the 8(a) program receive significant benefits, however.

Part of the reason for the lack of performance and impact of the 8(a) program rests on the effectiveness of efforts to characterize the minority business effort as "reverse discrimination." This successfully limited the number and types of companies eligible to participate in the program. Impact was also reduced by the fearfulness of government agencies and advocates, whose concern about being accused of discriminating against white business owners led them to reduce the usefulness of this program. The results of this inef-fectiveness can be seen in Federal contracting statistics. Small Black firms received 1.67% of Federal contracting dollars.

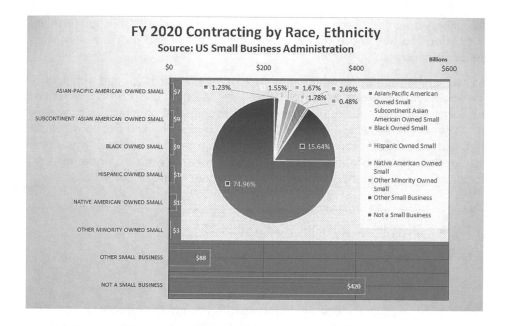

FY 2020 Contracting by Race, Ethnicity
Source: US Small Business Administration

Offices of Minority and Women Inclusion

One of the most overlooked but important provisions of Dodd-Frank requires federal financial institution regulatory agencies to examine diversity efforts at the 27,000 financial institutions 29 federal agencies regulate. (See www. officeofminorityandwomeninclusion.com for real-time information.)

Section 342 of the Dodd-Frank Wall Street Reform and Consumer Protection Act contains a provision creating an Office of Minority and Women Inclusion (OMWI) at 29 agencies. The Section requires the Department of the Treasury, the Federal Deposit Insurance Corporation (FDIC), the Federal Housing Finance Agency, each of the Federal Reserve Banks, the Board of Governors of the Federal Reserve System, the National Credit Union Administration, the Office of the Comptroller of the Currency, the Securities and Exchange Commission, and the Bureau of Consumer Financial Protection to create "an Office of Minority and Women Inclusion ('OMWI') to be responsible for all agency matters relating to diversity in management, employment and business activities."

While the success or failure of this effort rests on the level of scrutiny the agencies will apply to the financial institutions and the techniques they use, lawmakers assumed that knowing they are being watched will spur financial institutions to hire more minority employees and spend more money with minority contractors.[1]

As one analyst noted, "In addition to developing standards for and monitoring the employment diversity of the respective agency, the OMWI will have authority over the entities regulated by the agency and contractors providing services to the agencies." Service providers covered by the Section include "financial institutions, investment banking firms, mortgage banking firms, asset management firms, brokers, dealers, financial services entities, underwriters, accountants, investment consultants, and providers of legal services."

▉ SEC. 342. OFFICE OF MINORITY AND WOMEN INCLUSION.

(a) OFFICE OF MINORITY AND WOMEN INCLUSION.—

(1) ESTABLISHMENT.—

(A) IN GENERAL.—Except as provided in subparagraph (B), not later than 6 months after the date of enactment of this Act, each agency shall establish an Office of Minority and Women Inclusion that shall be responsible for all matters of the agency relating to diversity in management, employment, and business activities.

(B) BUREAU.—The Bureau shall establish an Office of Minority and Women Inclusion not later than 6 months after the designated transfer date established under section 1062.

1) IN GENERAL.—The Director of each Office shall be appointed by, and shall report to, the agency administrator. The position of Director shall be a career reserved position in the Senior Executive Service, as that position is defined in section 3132 of title 5, United States Code, or an equivalent designation.

(2) DUTIES.—Each Director shall develop standards for—

(A) equal employment opportunity and the racial, ethnic, and gender diversity of the workforce and senior management of the agency;

(B) increased participation of minority-owned and women-owned businesses in the programs and contracts of the agency, including standards for coordinating technical assistance to such businesses; and

(C) assessing the diversity policies and practices of entities regulated by the agency.

---

[1] Cunningham, "Dodd Frank 342 and Minority Firms," *The Washington Post,* June 5, 2011. Available at www.washingtonpost.com/business/capitalbusiness/commentary-new-law-a-boon-for-women--and-minority-owned-firms/2011/06/01/AGxHCfJH_story.html

(3) OTHER DUTIES.—Each Director shall advise the agency administrator on the impact of the policies and regulations of the agency on minority-owned and women-owned businesses. There are many national, state and local organizations focused on minority business development. We will list and evaluate these entities.

Minority-owned firms in general, according to the Small Business Administration (SBA), generate less revenue than their nonminority counterparts. For instance, black-owned businesses earn 43 cents for every dollar earned by white-owned firms, according to the SBA.

Moreover, a study conducted by the Commerce Department's Minority Business Development Agency concluded that women- and minority-owned firms "experience higher loan denial probabilities and pay higher interest rates than white-owned businesses even after controlling for differences in credit-worthiness, and other factors."[2] The failure rate of minority businesses is higher than that of nonminority firms, according to the study, partly because of lack of capital.

OMWI Offices

Table 3-1 lists Office of Minority and Women Inclusion (OMWI) offices and the administrator of each. For minority- and women-owned companies looking to grow, if you want to sell goods and services to the federal government, this table provides the names of persons you may wish to contact. (Note: The data in this table changes frequently. For updates, please visit www.officeofminorityandwomeninclusion.com for real-time information.)

Table 3-1. OMWI Offices and Administrators

Agency	Person Responsible for OMWI Office
Treasury – Domestic Finance OMWI_Team@Treasury.gov 202-927-8181	Lorraine Cole
Treasury – Economic Policy	Lorraine Cole
Treasury – General Counsel	Lorraine Cole
Treasury – International Affairs	Lorraine Cole

(continued)

[2] Robert W. Fairlie and Alicia M. Robb, *Disparities in Capital Access between Minority and Non-Minority-Owned Businesses: The Troubling Reality of Capital Limitations Faced by MBEs*, U.S. Department of Commerce, Minority Business Development Agency, January 2010: 21.

Table 3-1. (*continued*)

Agency	Person Responsible for OMWI Office
Treasury – Legislative Affairs	Lorraine Cole
Treasury – Management/CFO	Lorraine Cole
Treasury – Public Affairs	Lorraine Cole
Treasury – Tax Policy	Lorraine Cole
Treasury – Terrorism and Financial Intelligence (TFI)	Lorraine Cole
Treasury – Treasurer of the United States	Lorraine Cole
Federal Deposit Insurance Corporation	Claire N. Lam
3501 Fairfax Drive, Room E-2098, Arlington, VA 22226 Anthony Pagano at (703) 562-6062 or APagano@fdic.gov	
Federal Housing Finance Agency	Sharron P. A. Levine
OMWI: (202) 649-3806, OMWIinfo@fhfa.gov	
Federal Reserve Bank of Boston	Marques Benton
email marques.benton@bos.frb.org	
(617) 973-3153	
Federal Reserve Bank of New York	Diane Ashley
33 Liberty Street	
New York, NY 10045	
Tel: (212) 720-5000	
general.info@ny.frb.org	
Federal Reserve Bank of Philadelphia diversity@phil.frb.org	Mary Ann Hood
Federal Reserve Bank of Cleveland	Diana Starks
omwi@clev.frb.org	
Federal Reserve Bank of Chicago	Kathryn Medina
230 South LaSalle Street	
Chicago, Illinois 60604-1413	
(312) 322-5322	
www.chicagofed.org/utilities/contactus	
Federal Reserve Bank of St. Louis	Anna Hart
omwi@stls.frb.org	

(*continued*)

Table 3-1. (*continued*)

Agency	Person Responsible for OMWI Office
Federal Reserve Bank of Minneapolis	Michael Garrett
90 Hennepin Avenue	
Minneapolis, MN 55401	
(612) 204-5000. For media inquiries, contact Alyssa Augustine by email at Alyssa.Augustine@mpls.frb.org or phone at (612) 204-5175	
Federal Reserve Bank of Kansas City	Tammy Edwards
1 Memorial Drive	
Kansas City, Mo. 64198	
tammy.edwards@kc.frb.org	
Federal Reserve Bank of Dallas	Alison Schmidt
2200 N. Pearl St., Dallas, Texas 75201	
214.922.6000 or 800.333.4460	
Federal Reserve Bank of San Francisco sf.omwi@sf.frb.org	Rita Aguilar
(415) 974-2482	
Federal Reserve Bank of Richmond www.richmondfed.org/ contact_us/?mapid=9141204f-11fb-4b8d-95fb-8bbb68a00231&r=a453e4a0-92bb-4224-82fb-eb0a463cd8b5	Beth Panilaitis 804-697-5479
Federal Reserve Bank of Atlanta	Chapelle Dabney Davis
OMWI@atl.frb.org	
Board of Governors of the Federal Reserve System 20th Street and Constitution Avenue N.W., Washington, DC 20551	Shelia Clark
ODI-Section342-DiversityStandards@frb.gov	
National Credit Union Administration	Monica Davy
1775 Duke Street	
Alexandria, VA 22314	
703 518-1650	
omwimail@ncua.gov	
Office of the Comptroller of the Currency	Joyce Cofield
400 7th Street SW	
Washington, DC 20219	
(202) 649-6460	
omwi-outreach@occ.treas.gov	

(*continued*)

Table 3-1. (*continued*)

Agency	Person Responsible for OMWI Office
Securities and Exchange Commission 202-551-6046 omwi@sec.gov	Pamela Gibbs
Consumer Financial Protection Bureau OMWI@consumerfinance.gov	Lora McCray

The chart compares total agency contracting reported by each agency with an OMWI office in 2014 versus 2019.

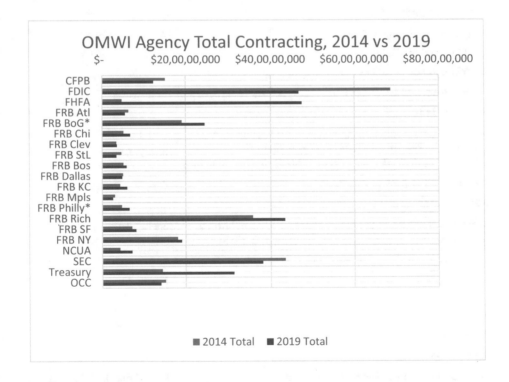

OMWI Offices

CFPB	Consumer Financial Protection Bureau
FDIC	Federal Deposit Insurance Corp.
FHFA	Federal Housing Finance Agency
FRB Atl	Federal Reserve Bank of Atlanta
FRB BoG*	Federal Reserve Board of Governors
FRB Chi	Federal Reserve Bank of Chicago
FRB Clev	Federal Reserve Bank of Cleveland
FRB StL	Federal Reserve Bank of St. Louis
FRB Bos	Federal Reserve Bank of Boston
FRB Dallas	Federal Reserve Bank of Dallas
FRB KC	Federal Reserve Bank of Kansas City
FRB Mpls	Federal Reserve Bank of Minneapolis
FRB Philly*	Federal Reserve Bank of Philadelphia
FRB Rich	Federal Reserve Bank of Richmond
FRB SF	Federal Reserve Bank of San Francisco
FRB NY	Federal Reserve Bank of New York
NCUA	National Credit Union Administration
SEC	Securities and Exchange Commission
Treasury	US Department of the Treasury
OCC	Office of the Comptroller of the Currency

The following chart shows the same data expressed as the difference in total contracting amounts for minority firms versus women-owned firms. It also shows the difference in total contracting dollars spent by these agencies.

We reviewed the performance of the OMWI offices from 2014 to 2019, based on annual reports these offices issue to Congress. Total contracting at agencies subject to OMWI increased from $2,872,716,865 in 2014 to $3,367,292,219 by 2019.

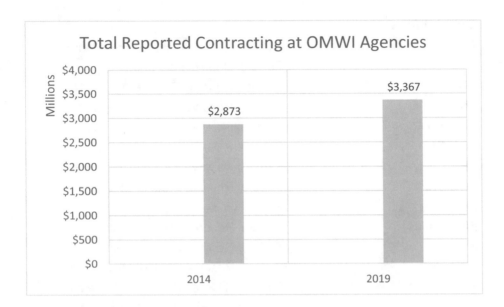

Contracts awarded to minority-owned firms grew from **$505,469,385** in 2014 to **$614,962,143** in 2019, a difference of **$109 million**. Contracts awarded to women-owned firms grew from **$323,382,575** in 2014 to **$465,080,469** in 2019, a difference of **$141,697,895**.

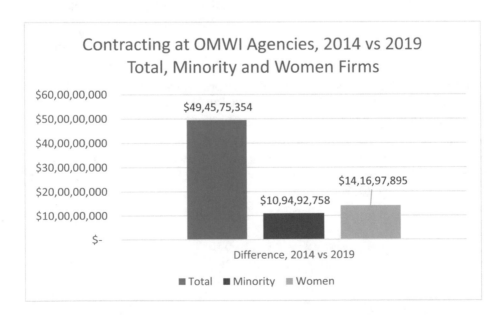

Firms owned by white women make up the majority of the Women business category listed earlier. Minority firms are defined as firms owned by men from the following ethnic groups: African American, Asian/Pacific Islander, Hispanic, Native American, and Multiethnic (more than one of the preceding categories).

Thus, the data shows that the bulk of the benefit from the growth in minority and women contracting at these agencies has gone to firms owned by white women.

As the figures and tables show, the federal government spends significant amounts of money with women and minority firms. If your firm meets this definition (51% or more of the common stock owned by women or minorities), you may wish to consider trying to do business with one or more of the agencies listed there.

As we have stated before, however, your chances of actually getting a contract with these entities are low. Strategies we have seen that increase your chances include working with or hiring former employees of the agency you are targeting and reaching out to local, state, and federal representatives for assistance.

Best and Worst Performing OMWI Offices

To save you time and money, we have provided in the following our review of the best and worst OMWI Offices:

- Consumer Financial Protection Bureau – The Office has not implemented several critical policies and lacks vision to tie the OMWI initiative to its mission. Minority contracting dollars have fallen as dollars to women firms have increased. D.

- Federal Deposit Insurance Corporation – The Agency lost its top rating with the passing of its former OMWI Director, Mickey Collins. They still do more minority contracting than any other OMWI Office Agency. B.

- Federal Housing Finance Agency – Getting better. C.

- Federal Reserve Board – Slowly improving. C.

- Federal Reserve Bank of Atlanta – No changes. C-.

- Federal Reserve Bank of Boston – Getting better. C.

- Federal Reserve Bank of Chicago – Limited African American contracting. D.

- Federal Reserve Bank of Cleveland – No changes. D.
- Federal Reserve Bank of Dallas – Better. C+.
- Federal Reserve Bank of Kansas City – Solid performer. C+.
- Federal Reserve Bank of Minneapolis – Solid performer. C+.
- Federal Reserve Bank of New York – Minimal social return. Elitist. D.
- Federal Reserve Bank of Philadelphia – N/A.
- Federal Reserve Bank of Richmond – Huge one-year jump in minority contracting. B+.
- Federal Reserve Bank of San Francisco – Troubling gap between potential and performance. C.
- Federal Reserve Bank of St. Louis – Large actual gap between potential and performance. D.
- Office of the Comptroller of the Currency – Had best performance in 2014. Moving rapidly in 2019. A-.

US Department of Transportation

A key set of minority business regulations came out of the US Department of Transportation. Federal highway, transit, airport, and highway safety contracting markets nationwide served as an early focus area in efforts to support minority businesses. In 1983, Congress "required the Department of Transportation (DOT) ensure that at least 10% of the funds authorized for the highway and transit Federal financial assistance programs be expended with" Disadvantaged Business Enterprises (DBEs), white-, women-, and minority-owned firms meeting the definitions established by the SBA 8(a) program.

The idea was that these projects and the companies selected to work on them provide an elevated level of job creation; that these projects often impacted minority, especially African American, communities; and that problems with explicit discrimination in the construction field made this area ripe for intervention.

Thus, the Department of Transportation's (DOT) Disadvantaged Business Enterprise (DBE) program was "designed to remedy ongoing discrimination and the continuing effects of past discrimination…the primary remedial goal and objective of the DBE program is to level the playing field by providing small businesses owned and controlled by socially and economically disadvantaged individuals a fair opportunity to compete for federally funded transportation contracts."

As with many Federal programs, the program's actual impact is limited to a small number of beneficiary minority companies. Given the reach and nature of the transportation construction industry, DOT programs influenced state and local minority business development efforts. DOT minority business "regulations require recipients of DOT Federal financial assistance, namely, state and local transportation agencies, to establish goals for the participation of disadvantaged entrepreneurs and certify the eligibility of DBE firms to participate in their DOT-assisted contracts."

■ **Department of Transportation** Minority and disadvantaged business participation. 49 U.S. Code § 47113

(a) Definitions.—In this section—

(1) "small business concern"—

(A) has the meaning given the term in section 3 of the Small Business Act (15 U.S.C. 632); but

(B) in the case of a concern in the construction industry, a concern shall be considered a small business concern if the concern meets the size standard for the North American Industry Classification System Code 237310, as adjusted by the Small Business Administration;

(2) "socially and economically disadvantaged individual" has the same meaning given that term in section 8(d) of the Act (15 U.S.C. 637(d)) and relevant subcontracting regulations prescribed under section 8(d), except that women are presumed to be socially and economically disadvantaged; and

(3) the term "qualified HUBZone small business concern" has the meaning given that term in section 31(b) of the Small Business Act.

(b) General Requirement.—

Except to the extent the Secretary decides otherwise, at least 10 percent of amounts available in a fiscal year under section 48103 of this title shall be expended with small business concerns owned and controlled by socially and economically disadvantaged individuals or qualified HUBZone small business concerns.

(c) Uniform Criteria.—

The Secretary shall establish minimum uniform criteria for State governments and airport sponsors to use in certifying whether a small business concern qualifies under this section. The criteria shall include on-site visits, personal interviews, licenses, analyses of stock ownership and bonding capacity, listings of equipment and work completed, resumes of principal owners, financial capacity, and type of work preferred.

(d) Surveys and Lists.—

Each State or airport sponsor annually shall survey and compile a list of small business concerns referred to in subsection (b) of this section and the location of each concern in the State.

(e) Mandatory Training Program.—

(1) In general.—

Not later than 1 year after the date of enactment of this subsection, the Secretary shall establish a mandatory training program for persons described in paragraph (3) to provide streamlined training on certifying whether a small business concern qualifies as a small business concern owned and controlled by socially and economically disadvantaged individuals under this section and section 47107(e).

(2) Implementation.—

The training program may be implemented by one or more private entities approved by the Secretary.

(3) Participants.—A person referred to in paragraph (1) is an official or agent of an airport sponsor—

(A) who is required to provide a written assurance under this section or section 47107(e) that the airport owner or operator will meet the percentage goal of subsection (b) of this section or section 47107(e)(1), as the case may be; or

(B) who is responsible for determining whether or not a small business concern qualifies as a small business concern owned and controlled by socially and economically disadvantaged individuals under this section or section 47107(e).

(Pub. L. 103–272, § 1(e), July 5, 1994, 108 Stat. 1268; Pub. L. 103–429, § 6(65), Oct. 31, 1994, 108 Stat. 4386; Pub. L. 105–135, title VI, § 604(h)(2), Dec. 2, 1997, 111 Stat. 2635; Pub. L. 112–95, title I, § 140(b), Feb. 14, 2012, 126 Stat. 27; Pub. L. 115–91, div. A, title XVII, § 1701(a)(4)(G)(ii), Dec. 12, 2017, 131 Stat. 1796; Pub. L. 115–254, div. B, title I, § 150, title V, § 539(o), Oct. 5, 2018, 132 Stat. 3215, 3371.)

Minority Business Development Agency

The US Department of Commerce Minority Business Development Agency (MBDA) was created by Executive Order 11458 to support the growth of minority-owned businesses in the United States. MBDA began as the Nixon Administration's Office of Minority Business Enterprises (OMBE).

■ Executive Order 11458   PRESCRIBING ARRANGEMENTS FOR DEVELOPING AND COORDINATING A NATIONAL PROGRAM FOR MINORITY BUSINESS ENTERPRISE

By virtue of the authority vested in me as President of the United States, it is ordered as follows:

SECTION 1. Functions of the Secretary of Commerce. (a) The Secretary of Commerce (hereinafter referred to as 'the Secretary') shall--

(1) Coordinate as consistent with law the plans, programs, and operations of the Federal Government which affect or may contribute to the establishment, preservation and strengthening of minority business enterprise.

(2) Promote the mobilization of activities and resources of State and local governments, businesses and trade associations, universities, foundations, professional organizations and volunteer and other groups towards the growth of minority business enterprises and facilitate the coordination of the efforts of these groups with those of Federal departments and agencies.

(3) Establish a center for the development, collection, summarization and dissemination of information that will be helpful to persons and organizations throughout the nation in undertaking or promoting the establishment and successful operation of minority business enterprises.

(b) The Secretary, as he deems necessary or appropriate to enable him to better fulfill the responsibilities vested in him by subsection (a), may--

(1) Develop, with the participation of other Federal departments and agencies as appropriate, comprehensive plans of Federal action and propose such changes in Federal programs as may be required.

(2) Require the submission of information from such departments and agencies necessary for him to carry out the purposes of this order.

(3) Convene for purposes of coordination meetings of the heads of such departments and agencies, or their designees, whose programs and activities may affect or contribute to the purposes of this order.

(4) Convene business leaders, educators, and other representatives of the private sector engaged in assisting the development of minority business enterprise or who could contribute to its development to propose, evaluate, and coordinate governmental and private activities in furtherance of the objectives of this order.

(5) Confer with and advise officials of State and local governments.

(6) Provide the managerial and organizational framework through which joint or collaborative undertakings with Federal departments or agencies or private organizations can be planned and implemented.

(7) Recommend appropriate legislative or executive actions.

SEC. 2. Establishment of the Advisory Council for Minority Enterprise. (a) There is hereby established the Advisory Council for Minority Enterprise (hereinafter referred to as 'the Council').

(b) The Council shall be composed of members appointed by the President from among persons, including members of minority groups and representatives from minority business enterprises, knowledgeable and dedicated to the purposes of this order. The members shall serve for a term of two years and may be reappointed.

(c) The President shall designate one of the members of the Council as the Chairman of the Council.

(d) The Council shall meet at the call of the Secretary.

(e) The Council shall be advisory to the Secretary in which capacity it shall--

(1) Serve as a source of knowledge and information on developments in different fields and segments of our economic and social life which affect minority business enterprise.

(2) Keep abreast of plans, programs and activities in the public and private sectors which relate to minority business enterprise, and advise the Secretary on any measures to better achieve the objectives of this order.

(3) Consider, and advise the Secretary and such officials as he may designate on, problems and matters referred to the Council.

(f) For the purposes of Executive Order No. 11007 of February 26, 1962, the Council shall be deemed to have been formed by the Secretary.

(g) Members of the Council shall be entitled to receive travel and expenses, including per diem in lieu of subsistence, as authorized by law (5 U.S.C. 5701- 5708) for persons in the Government service employed intermittently.

(h) The Secretary shall arrange for administrative support of the Council to the extent necessary including use of any gifts or bequests accepted by the Department of Commerce pursuant to law.

SEC. 3. Responsibilities of other Federal departments and agencies. (a) The head of each Federal department and agency, or a representative designated by him, when so requested by the Secretary, shall, to the extent permitted by law and funds available, furnish information and assistance, and participate in all ways appropriate to carry out the objectives of this order.

(b) The head of each Federal department or agency shall, when so requested by the Secretary, designate a senior official to have primary and continuing responsibility for the participation and cooperation of that department or agency in matters concerning minority business enterprise and activities as required by this order.

(c) The head of each Federal department or agency, or his designated representative, shall keep the Secretary informed of all proposed budgets, plans, and programs of his department or agency affecting minority business enterprise.

SEC. 4. Construction. Nothing in this order shall be construed as subjecting any function vested by law in, or assigned pursuant to law to, any Federal department or agency or head thereof to the authority of any other agency or officer, or as abrogating or restricting any such function in any manner.

Richard Nixon

THE WHITE HOUSE,

March 5, 1969.

Exec. Order No. 11458, 34 FR 4937, 1969 WL 9645 (Pres.)

MBDA's main role today is the provision of services through 40 "business centers." These centers provide consulting and advisory services, but not capital, to minority firms.

The following chart shows the number of Black firms created from 1972 to 2012 versus the amount of money allocated to MBDA. While MBDA's budget has decreased, the number of Black firms has grown dramatically. This suggests MBDA has limited impact on the creation of minority firms. Other factors, like demographics, may have been responsible for the growth in Black firms.

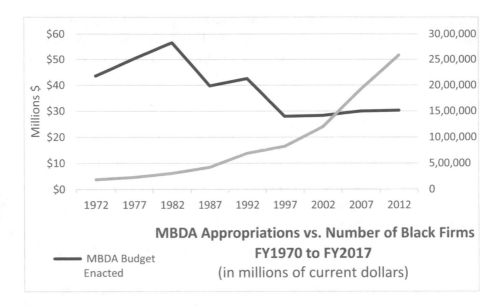

MBDA Appropriations vs. Number of Black Firms FY1970 to FY2017
(in millions of current dollars)

Based on performance and the current state of Black and minority businesses, OMBE and MBDA were and are largely symbolic, with no real authority, dedicated budget, or power to directly expand access to wealth and capital. This continues to this day: MBDA makes no loans and, as noted earlier, provides no capital to minority firms.

We note that, on August 5, 2021, the US Senate voted to make MBDA permanent and to create the position of Undersecretary of Commerce for Minority Business Development. While not encoded into law yet, if you are a minority-owned business, this is a development you will want to monitor.

Using This Chapter

Many laws have been enacted to support minority- and women-owned businesses. That these firms are still underperforming as a group says less about those firms and more about the intractable nature of racism and white supremacy in the United States. This chapter has provided a summary review of a small portion of the laws governing minority business support efforts in the United States. It is not meant to be comprehensive.

We also provided information on one of the most recent minority business support efforts, the Offices of Minority and Women Inclusion.

Our suggestion remains the same: develop a community-based, collaborative, cooperative approach to these laws and offices.

What to do:

1. Read the laws. As I said, this listing is not comprehensive, it serves as a starting point. Nothing is worse than reaching out to agencies and seeking to use these laws and initiatives without being informed about what the laws and regulations actually say. That's why we have reproduced many of them here.

2. Reach out to the OMWI Offices. Let them know who you are and what you do. Just be cognizant of the fact that it is extremely unlikely that you will *ever get a dime out of any of these offices*. They may be able to put you in touch with others in your region or industry, however, and, as a last resort, you might ask for help with problems you are sure to have with financial institutions. Just don't count on it.

3. Reach out to the House Financial Services Committee. The United States House Committee on Financial Services…is the committee of the House of Representatives that "oversees the entire financial services industry, including the securities, insurance, banking and housing industries." The Committee also oversees and manages the federal government's relationship with the following agencies:

Financial Services Agencies

US Department of the Treasury – www.treas.gov

Consumer Financial Protection Bureau – www.consumerfinance.gov

Federal Reserve – www.federalreserve.gov

Federal Deposit Insurance Corporation – www.fdic.gov

Office of the Comptroller of the Currency – www.occ.gov

Securities and Exchange Commission – www.sec.gov

US Department of Housing and Urban Development – www.hud.gov

National Credit Union Administration – www.ncua.gov

Federal Housing Finance Agency – www.fhfa.gov

US Government Accountability Office – www.gao.gov

Export-Import Bank – www.exim.gov

US Mint – www.usmint.gov

Bureau of Engraving and Printing – www.moneyfactory.gov

Financial Crimes Enforcement Network (FinCEN) – www.fincen.gov

And the following international and multilateral organizations:

World Bank – www.worldbank.org

International Monetary Fund (IMF) – www.imf.org

African Development Bank – www.afdb.org

Asian Development Bank – www.adb.org

European Bank for Reconstruction and Development – www.ebrd.com

Inter-American Development Bank – www.iadb.org

The Committee "is one of the House's most powerful committees" and is currently chaired by Democrat Maxine Waters from California.

Let them know who you are, what you do, and how you might be able to work with these agencies. Oftentimes, the agencies listed claim that they "cannot find qualified minority contractors." Of course, we know that is nonsense, but to foreclose any temptation on the part of the agencies to use that tired old excuse, you still have to reach out to them directly.

US House Committee on Financial Services Democrats

2129 Rayburn House Office Building

Washington, DC 20515

Phone: (202) 225-4247

Fax: (202) 225-6952

Email: FSCDems@mail.house.gov

https://financialservices.house.gov

4.   Contact your Congressional delegation. The goal is the same as before: let them know who you are and what you do. A word of caution: Don't expect that they will get you a contract or funding. Don't even ask. This will get you kicked out of Congressional and legislative office quickly (google ACORN 2009 undercover videos controversy). This is more about supporting your state, local, fraternal, faith-based, or ethnic community, keeping them informed about actual business conditions.

5. Join with others in your city, county, state, or region to reach out. Minority Chambers of Commerce, industry groups, fraternal organizations, church, and faith-based associations. Develop whatever relationships and you can, just don't be selfish or greedy. Collaborate.

6. Extreme collaboration. Take it a step further. Develop new highly collaborative strategies and techniques. At this time, sharing contacts, contracts, and, potentially, revenue is the way out of the current crisis.

It is our belief that all of the laws and regulations needed to significantly enhance minority businesses are in place. They are simply, for reasons that include bigotry, sexism, incompetence, selfishness, greed, corruption, and fear, unenforced.

Hopefully, recent events will spur renewed progress. If so, at least you'll be informed about prior laws and regulations.

Public Sector Institutions

Federal, State, and Local Minority Business Programs

Federal, state, and local governments have long recognized the value of women- and minority-owned firms. We've seen a resurgence of activity and interest in these offices during the pandemic.[1] Several (but not all) have expanded the resources and opportunities they offer for women- and minority-owned firms, and small businesses, to grow and to compete for both private sector and government contracts.

In this chapter, you will find information on state and local women and minority business agencies. We also include information on how to register as a state and/or local contractor. Once you have done so, you may be able to bid on federal, state, and local loan and government contracting opportunities.

[1] "The Small Business Development Center discusses the importance of aiding local businesses."https://wbng.com/2020/12/08/the-small-business-development-center-discusses-the-importance-of-aiding-local-businesses/

© William Michael Cunningham 2021
W. M. Cunningham, *Thriving As a Minority-Owned Business in Corporate America*,
https://doi.org/10.1007/978-1-4842-7240-4_4

While these opportunities appear attractive, a word of warning: discrimination against women and minorities in government lending programs is well documented.[2] (You know this. You wouldn't be reading this book if you did not. You're also not going to let this stop you. I understand. Read on.)

More importantly, the vast majority of women- and minority-owned firms never receive a federal, state, or local government contract and are unlikely to receive one. Depending upon your industry, government contracting opportunities vary. So few minority firms ever get a government contract that, unless you have special ties or connections, we would not look to the government, ANY government, to be your first customer.

Regardless, these agencies and institutions can assist you in establishing and, possibly, growing your woman- or minority-owned business. Our advice boils down to this: *use the ones that work; don't use the ones that don't.* You can tell the difference by doing a little research. There are a number of forums and resources that provide accurate, real-time evaluations of these resources. Talk to community groups, Chambers of Commerce, and minority business groups. Typically, they will know who is doing a good job for their members. Look online. (There should be a Yelp-like rating service to tell which of these agencies actually get money to minority firms and which do not....) These organizations will also be sensitive to the political environment, including recent government budgets. (If they aren't, look for another group.) Look for ways to effectively and efficiently utilize federal, state, and local programs to help your firm any way you can.

Just understand that, while there are questions about effectiveness, you still need to know these agencies, programs, and resources exist.

State Offices of Women- and Minority-Owned Businesses

Several states have agencies dedicated to helping women- and minority-owned businesses. Most focus on the provision of technical and, in some limited form, financial assistance. The goal is to help these firms successfully compete for federal, state, and local government and commercial contracts. You can find a list here:

www.mbda.gov/page/state-offices-minority-and-women-business-enterprises

---

[2] "Disparities In Government Contracting Hurt Minority-Owned Businesses." NPR. February 20, 2020 5:00 AM ET. www.npr.org/2020/02/20/807126443/disparities-in-government-contracting-hurt-minority-owned-businesses

As we noted in prior chapters, relative to the large number of women and minority firms, very few obtain contracts, however. The majority of minority-owned firms simply do not. Therefore, we suggest you view these federal and state agencies as general resources. If they help you get a contract or financing, fine.

Focus on other types of support and assistance these offices offer. With the focus on small, local, and minority firms resulting from the pandemic, many of these agencies have stepped up their minority business game.

Certification As a Women- or Minority-Owned Firm

One of the services these offices may be able to provide is woman or minority firm *certification*. As defined before, federal, state, and local governments define women or minority firms as one owned by a person or people who are Women, African American, Alaskan Native, American Indian, Asian American, or Hispanic. Members from these groups must own and control 51% of the firm's common stock (if any) and also must control the firm's day-to-day operations.

■ **MBE Certification**   Federal, state, and local programs require **certification that confirms minority or women ownership of a firm** – this is a formal evaluation and review process to confirm the minority or women ownership of a company. Only businesses owned by women or minorities are eligible for MBE Program consideration. Typically, once certified, the women- or minority-owned business is awarded a certificate. We have included a sample certification form in the appendix.

Certification can be a lengthy process. The documentation required is extensive, as confirmed by the minority business documentation requirements for the State of Alabama, as follows:

    A. State of Alabama Department of Finance vendor registration (if a registered vendor)

    B. Articles of Incorporation, or Organization, if an LLC

    C. Stock or membership certificate for each business owner/ stock holder

    D. Other certifications (DBE, M/WBE, etc.), as applicable

E. Statement of duties for each stockholder or business owner

F. Current Alabama state, city, and/or county business license

G. Professional license, as applicable

H. Federal and state income tax returns for the previous two years

I. Bank signature card

J. Capability Statement (ability to produce other products or services)

K. Brief history of business entity

L. Picture of business facility (building signage, office area, etc.)

M. Proof of citizenship (ID card, tribal card, or citizenship papers if naturalized citizen).

N. Picture ID of each business owner (e.g., driver's license)

These requirements are extreme. They have been put into place due to fears of *MBE certification fraud*, defined as nonminority firms and individuals registering as minority in order to gain government contracts or to gain some other economic benefit. The highpoint of this type of fraud occurred decades ago, as MBE programs were first adopted. So few meaningful MBE programs exist today that the level of meaningful MBE fraud has decreased significantly, but, like other forms of fictional fraud supposedly carried out by minorities (voting, for example), the idea that false MBE registration occurs is still prevalent. Hence the extreme, burdensome, and unhelpful certification requirements.

In addition to being extensive, WBE and MBE recertification tends to be required on an annual basis. Still, depending upon your industry, the process may very well be worth it. We anticipate that new certification processes using social media assets and other new data tools to verify the identity will be utilized in the future.

To start, we suggest you look for self-certification options. If you have a listing on Facebook or Yelp, you can self-certify as a Black or minority firm.

Yelp Teams Up with My Black Receipt to Support Black-owned Businesses

Tara Lewis, VP of Community Expansion + Trends. Thursday, June 18, 2020 • #Product, #Impact, #News

"Today, we're excited to officially launch the Black-owned business attribute in partnership with My Black Receipt, a movement whose mission is to empower the Black community with economic independence by galvanizing consumers to spend $5 million at Black-owned businesses from Juneteenth (June 19) through Independence Day (July 4). The new searchable Black-owned business attribute is free and opt-in only, as the decision to self-identify as Black-owned should rest solely with the business."

Facebook announced a similar effort. See `www.facebook.com/business/news/support-black-owned-business`.

We have included a sample self-certification form in the appendix.

I would always follow up with more formal, external certification, however. But, most who register as minority businesses are, in fact, minority businesses.

See `www.bmc.com/content/dam/bmc/corporate/supplier-diversity-self-cert.pdf` for an example of a self-certification form. After gaining traction, apply for more formal certification through the SBA. See `https://certify.sba.gov/`.

State Woman and Minority Business Certification Offices

The following link lists state offices supporting women and minority business certification:

`www.ncsl.org/research/labor-and-employment/minority-business-development.aspx`

Federal Resources

The US Small Business Administration (SBA) was created to support small businesses and entrepreneurs. The agency offered several loan programs in the face of the COVID crisis. These included the Paycheck Protection Program and the Economic Injury Disaster Loan Emergency Advance (EIDL) Program.

Many of these have expired, but SBA still offers the SBA Economic Injury Disaster Loan (EIDL) Program on a more permanent basis, which provides low-interest loans for eligible small businesses.

For minority firms, especially Black firms, the programs put into place to deal with the economic downturn were less effective. In a national survey of small businesses we conducted in April 2020 on the Paycheck Protection Program and the Economic Injury Disaster Loan Emergency Advance (EIDL) Program, out of the 60% of survey respondents who applied for the PPP program, 33% got some level of funding. Of the 72% of the survey respondents who applied to the EIDL program, 28% got some level of funding. Ninety-one percent (91%) of survey respondents were Black Americans.[3]

On October 15, 2020, news reports surfaced that Wells Fargo, a major bank responsible for the distribution of SBA program funding "fired more than 100 employees, saying they personally defrauded a coronavirus relief program from the U.S. Small Business Administration."[4]

Factors like this make easy for some to doubt the effectiveness of SBA programs. Others question if these agencies will ever be truly effective for women and minority firms. Still, the Agency offers other relevant resources. They offer classes on relevant business topics, can get you face to face with free business counselors through SCORE, and can help with minority business certification via https://certify.sba.gov/, cited earlier in this chapter.

The Agency has offices around the country and works with a number of affiliates. You can find a list of SBA District Offices at this link:

www.sba.gov/about-sba/sba-locations

Small Business Development Centers

Small Business Development Centers (SBDCs) are administered by the SBA and provide help to current and soon-to-be business owners. They do so by supplying information and free advice to individuals and small businesses via roughly 900 service centers. Sixty-two of these serve as "Lead Centers." Lead Centers sponsor other locations, service centers, within a State or region. Service centers, in turn, are "located at colleges, universities, community colleges, vocational schools, chambers of commerce and economic development corporations."

---

[3] Black American Business Owners Sound Off in New Survey of PPP Programs. www.blackenterprise.com/black-american-business-owners-sound-off-in-new-survey-of-ppp-programs/
[4] Wells Fargo Fires More Than 100 Employees Accused Of Coronavirus Relief Fraud. www.npr.org/sections/coronavirus-live-updates/2020/10/15/923976874/wells-fargo-fires-more-than-100-employees-for-alleged-coronavirus-relief-fraud

The SBDC program puts private sector organizations, educational institutions, and federal, state, and local governments together. It's a good resource to be aware of and a good place to start (or continue) your journey.

SBDC locations are listed at www.creativeinvest.com.

To get updates, visit www.sba.gov/local-assistance/find?type=Small%20 Business%20Development%20Center&pageNumber=1.

Department of Agriculture

The Department of Agriculture (USDA) helps agricultural producers, including minority producers. As with other Federal programs, the effectiveness of these efforts with respect to minority firms has long been questioned.[5] Still, if you are in this sector, you will need the help of the Department of Agriculture. More information can be found at www.farmers.gov/.

Relevant resources include the Rural Development Business programs:

- Business and Industry Loan Guarantees (B&I)
- Energy Programs
- Higher Blends Infrastructure Incentive Program
- Intermediary Relending Program (IRP)
- Rural Business Development Grants (RBDG)
- Rural Business Investment Program (RBIP)
- Rural Cooperative Development Grants (RCDG)
- Rural Economic Development Loan and Grant (REDLG)
- Rural Microentrepreneur Assistance Program (RMAP)
- Socially Disadvantaged Group Grants (SDGG)
- Value Added Producer Grants (VAPG)

---

[5] See Timothy Pigford, et al., v. Dan Glickman, Secretary, United States Department of Agriculture, US District Court for the District of Columbia, Civil Action No. 97-1978 (PLF). Paul L. Friedman, U.S. District Judge. "Pigford v. Glickman (1999) was a class action lawsuit against the United States Department of Agriculture (USDA), alleging racial discrimination against African-American farmers in its allocation of farm loans and assistance." https://en.wikipedia.org/wiki/Pigford_v._Glickman

Department of Housing and Urban Development

As noted by HUD, "The Community Development Block Grant (CDBG) Program provides annual grants on a formula basis to states, cities, and counties to develop viable urban communities by providing decent housing and a suitable living environment, and by expanding economic opportunities, principally for low- and moderate-income persons. The program is authorized under Title 1 of the Housing and Community Development Act of 1974, Public Law 93-383, as amended 42 U.S.C.-530.1 et seq."

While the CDBG Program supports "low- and moderate-income persons," many of whom are women or minority, it has no direct lending or financing programs for women or minority firms, but it is entirely possible that States and local governments may use CDBG funds for this propose. This, of course, adds another level of bureaucracy. We list it here because, as you dig deeper into minority business resources, eventually you will be referred to the program, but, again, it is not of direct relevance.

Department of the Treasury

The Treasury's Community Development Financial Institutions (CDFI) Fund was created to provide financial support to financial institutions that work with community businesses. The Fund offers a number of current and recent programs, including the New Markets Tax Credit Program. As with all of the Federal programs cited, there have been questions concerning the effectiveness of CDFI programs. According to a report issued by the Government Accountability Office (GAO), "From 2005 through 2008, minority-owned CDEs were successful with about 9 percent of the NMTC applications that they submitted to the CDFI Fund and received about $354 million of the $8.7 billion for which they applied, or about 4 percent. By comparison, nonminority CDEs were successful with about 27 percent of their applications and received $13.2 billion of the $89.7 billion for which they applied, or about 15 percent."

As with other programs cited, we feel it is important for minority firms to know about these efforts and to use them where and when they can. Start by visiting www.cdfifund.gov/. Visit www.minorityfinance.com/cdfis.html.

There are a number of CDFI trade associations. See https://cdfi.org/ for more information.

The Federal Reserve System

The Federal Reserve's 2020 Small Business Credit Survey (SBCS)[6] reported that

> *Key performance indicators declined substantially for the majority of employer firms between 2019 and 2020. Firms owned by people of color were more likely to report that they reduced business operations in response to the COVID-19 pandemic. Sixty-seven percent of Asian and Black-owned firms reported reducing their operations, followed by 63% of Hispanic-owned firms and 54% of white-owned firms.*

To support small- and medium-sized firms, including minority-owned firms, the Federal Reserve established an indirect lending facility, the Main Street Lending Program (MSLP). According to the Fed, MSLP operates through five facilities:

- the Main Street New Loan Facility (MSNLF),

- the Main Street Priority Loan Facility (MSPLF),

- the Main Street Expanded Loan Facility (MSELF),

- the Nonprofit Organization New Loan Facility (NONLF), and

- the Nonprofit Organization Expanded Loan Facility (NOELF).

Like many of the programs cited here, this is an indirect lending[7] program, operating via financial institutions. Businesses and nonprofits eligible for financing under this facility "must have no more than 15,000 employees or had no more than \$5 billion in revenue in 2019." There are several other eligibility requirements, which can be reviewed at www.bostonfed.org/mslp-faqs and www.bostonfed.org/-/media/Documents/special-lending-facilities/mslp/legal/frequently-asked-questions-faqs-nonprofit.pdf.

---

[6] The Federal Reserve System. SMALL BUSINESS CREDIT SURVEY. 2021 REPORT ON FIRMS OWNED BY PEOPLE OF COLOR. www.fedsmallbusiness.org/survey/2021/2021-report-on-firms-owned-by-people-of-color

[7] At the Federal Reserve Bank of Kansas City in 1994, we suggested the Federal Reserve Board's Federal Open Market Committee (FOMC) purchase mortgage-backed securities (MBS) originated by Black banks as part of open market operations. The Fed, then under Alan Greenspan, declined, saying that only Treasury securities were appropriate collateral. Since the financial crisis, the Fed has purchased trillions in securities, helping white-owned banks, broker-dealers, insurance companies, auto companies, and investment banks. We believe that the FOMC should create a social impact investment liquidity pool totaling at least \$50 billion by conducting repo and reverse repo transactions, purchasing Treasury, Energy Efficient MBS securities (and/or SBA PPP loans), and securities designed to reduce homelessness.

Economic Development Administration

The Economic Development Administration (EDA) is a branch of the Department of Commerce that administers a revolving loan fund (RLF) program. Loans are made by one of the approximately 400 organizations administering EDA-funded RLFs. You can find out more about EDA at www.eda.gov/pdf/about/EDA-trifold-2017.pdf.

To see which organizations are involved in the program, visit the EDA website: www.eda.gov/resources/.

As with the other Federal programs, this is an indirect lending program that has a spotty record of making resources available to women and minority firms. But, as with other programs listed in this chapter, you should know about these entities. Certainly, understanding the rules and regulations surrounding this program is a must.

Individuals are not eligible to receive assistance directly from EDA. To get assistance, you "must be a state, a political subdivision of a state, district organization, Indian tribe, institution of higher education, or a non-profit acting in coordination with a political subdivision of a state."

Projects must meet several criteria:

- *An unemployment rate that is, for the most recent twenty four (24) month period for which data are available, at least one (1) percentage point greater than the national average unemployment rate;*

- *Per capita income that is, for the most recent period for which data are available, eighty (80) percent or less of the national average per capita income;*

- *Or a "special need" (certain unemployment or economic adjustment issues, such as a presidentially-declared disaster, as determined by EDA).*

You can find a listing of economic development resources supported by EDA at www.eda.gov/resources/directory/.

Minority Business Development Agency

The Minority Business Development Agency (MBDA) is the Federal government's main agency dedicated to supporting women- and minority-owned firms. As with just about every other program, they do no direct lending, but operate through other institutions, in this case, a group of business development centers. These centers provide services to minority-owned firms. You can find a list of these centers on our websites, www.minorityfinance.com and www.creativeinvest.com.

National Institute of Standards and Technology, Manufacturing Extension Partnership

One of the most unique minority business partnerships is the National Institute of Standards and Technology's Manufacturing Extension Partnership. The Partnership helps manufacturers to offer custom services for small- and medium-sized manufacturers. The idea behind the partnership is to create a platform for innovation while at the same time allowing smaller manufacturers to survive and thrive. The Program also seeks to improve manufacturing efficiency and production processes.

This type of initiative is welcome: imagine having the capacity to manufacture, say, masks in the United States, instead of having to get them from China. This is the type of capability this program seeks to provide.

It goes without saying, however, that women and minority manufacturing firms will have to clear additional hurdles, since the perception in this market is that minority-owned firms do not have the capacity to participate. As with many other falsehoods, we know this is untrue.

GovLoans.gov

A Federal website, GovLoans.gov offers detail on government loan programs. The site is completely free. Use the site's Loan Finder questionnaire to receive a list of loans you may be eligible for.

As one Federal Reserve study noted, "more than half of companies that have black owners were turned down for loans, a rate twice as high as white business owners."[8]

Given the above, for women and minority firms, bank loans, even government-backed bank loans, may not be the first or even the third best source. The best first source is always family and friends. A second source might be crowdfunding.

---

[8] "Black-owned firms are twice as likely to be rejected for loans. Is this discrimination?" *The Guardian*. Thu 16 Jan 2020. www.theguardian.com/business/2020/jan/16/black-owned-firms-are-twice-as-likely-to-be-rejected-for-loans-is-this-discrimination

Crowdfunding

Crowdfunding works by allowing an entrepreneur with an idea for a company or product to post the details of the idea or product on a website such as Kickstarter or Indiegogo.

Dawn Dickson ✔️
@THEDawnDickson

I learned about crowdfunding at the 2014
@blackenterprise
Entrepreneur Summit from Bill Cunningham
@Creativelnv - he was talking about the JOBS Act early,
that sparked my initial interest and led to me being the
first female founder to raise over $1M by equity
crowdfunding

11:14 AM · Jul 10, 2020 · Twitter Web App

4 Retweets **52** Likes

Creative Investment Research @Creativelnv · 17h
Replying to @THEDawnDickson and @blackenterprise
Thank you and congratulations. We always had faith in you!

This is one of the only viable ways Black companies can get funded independently, as detailed in my books on the subject: *Top 50 Crowdfunding Campaigns: Fifty Most Successful Crowdfunding Campaigns* at www.amazon.com/dp/B00RKK4NL0 and *The JOBS Act: Crowdfunding for Small Businesses and Startups* at www.amazon.com/JOBS-Act-Crowdfunding-Businesses-Startups/dp/143024755X/.

Digital Currency

Digital currency, like Bitcoin or Ethereum, may be the third choice: in 2017, we suggested a group of Black women entrepreneurs buy bitcoin. It was $1700 then. It grew to $56,000 by April 2021. This might be enough to start a business. (See: Using Bitcoin to Finance Black Women https://youtu.be/5T0OrJe0hKM via @YouTube.) Keep in mind: this performance is unlikely to happen again, and digital currencies like Bitcoin are extremely risky. It might just as easily go to $0. Never risk more than you can afford to lose. I discuss this option in greater detail in Chapter 6.

For a quick review, please take our free class: Bitcoin and Blockchain Explained IN 30 MINUTES – Understanding Bitcoin and Blockchain. www.udemy.com/course/bitcoin-explained/.

Credit Unions

Finally, credit unions remain a viable option. Credit unions are member-owned financial institutions operating as cooperatives. They are managed by members and operate on the principle of people helping people. Credit unions seek to provide members credit and other financial services at competitive rates.

The "people helping people" focus of the institutions has certain performance benefits: they "had one-fifth the failure rate of other banks during the financial crisis of 2007–2008 and more than doubled lending to small businesses between 2008 and 2016, from $30 billion to $60 billion … lending to small businesses overall during the same period declined by around $100 billion." Also, "small businesses are eighty percent less likely to be dissatisfied with a credit union than with a big bank."

For a listing of minority-owned credit unions in the United States, see www.minorityfinance.com/creditunions.html.

Business Networking

National and International Chambers of Commerce and Major Supplier Diversity Organizations

One of the keys to helping your minority business survive any crisis is information (like this book). One way to get accurate, impactful information is through networking.[1] Many private sector organizations provide guidance and networking opportunities to women- and minority-owned firms. Of course, there has been an explosion in minority business databases, websites, and other resources. While I will do an in-depth review and analysis of these resources in the next chapter, I start the process here. I will also provide advice on how these resources can help.

---

[1] Networking is defined as "the action or process of interacting with others to exchange information and develop professional or social contacts."

© William Michael Cunningham 2021
W. M. Cunningham, *Thriving As a Minority-Owned Business in Corporate America*,
https://doi.org/10.1007/978-1-4842-7240-4_5

This chapter describes Chambers of Commerce and gives you information you can use to establish, promote, and grow your business.

Chambers of Commerce Supporting Women- and/or Minority-Owned Firms

A Chamber of Commerce is a business support organization (Figure 5-1). They exist to make life easier for businesses and the people who run them. Theoretically, this translates into economic benefits for society. For women- and minority-owned firms, this type of business support can be very helpful.

Figure 5-1. Texas Association of African American Chambers of Commerce, 2015

Exchanging information about the general business climate and opportunities (or the lack thereof) can help minority business owners, in particular, avoid certain gender- or race-related problems. In the midst of a national crisis, information flows are particularly important, especially accurate data on government and private sector assistance.

■ **Chambers of Commerce**   Chambers of Commerce are business networking organizations. They exist to represent the interest of businesses and business owners, either on a state, local, or industry basis. They also organize on a demographic basis: there are Asian Chambers, Black Chambers, Hispanic Chambers, and Women Business Chambers.

This gets to one of the keys for productive participation in these types of organizations. You need to be sure that institutions and larger businesses that support these chambers actually have the interest of the community you belong to first and foremost. Note that this does not mean these supporting organizations have to be perfect; after all, I gave a talk sponsored, in part, by Wells Fargo, a company I have criticized for damaging the Black community.[2] It does mean that you should look for Chambers that are independently funded and self-sustaining. There are very few of these in the minority community, but asking questions is important, since the benefits you receive from these business support organizations may very well depend upon having independent and objective staff and management. If that doesn't exist in your region, you may want to create a Chamber that meets these standards. This gets to another key: your active participation is required if you are to benefit fully.

Figure 5-2. Presentation Notice: Dallas Black Chamber of Commerce, 2017

---

[2] In my defense, they keep doing stupid things. See "Time to clean house at Wells Fargo." American Banker Newspaper. November 20, 2018, 10:26 a.m. EST. www.americanbanker. com/opinion/time-to-clean-house-at-wells-fargo

Why Join a Chamber of Commerce?

There are several benefits to joining a Chamber of Commerce, especially one tied to members of your ethnic or gender group.

We discussed minority business certification in an earlier chapter. Joining an ethnic (Asian, Black, Hispanic, Native American, or Women-focused) Chamber is a quick and easy way to self-certify without going through the burdensome and intrusive formal minority business certification process. *Note: Not all members of an ethnic Chamber of Commerce are also members of the relevant minority group, but most, in fact, are.* While membership in a minority chamber will not be enough to qualify formally for minority business validation, it is a quick way to self-certify. In addition, by joining a Chamber and networking with minority firms that have gone through the formal certification process, you can determine if the certification process is worth it.

Many Chambers are actively involved in local, state, and national public policy discussions concerning minority business activity. Topics include business certification policies; federal, state, and local taxes; minority business contracting; set-asides; and, of course, small business financing.

It's also a good way to learn about new financing tools and techniques. For example, we were instrumental in getting crowdfunding legislation offered – and passed – by former Texas State Representative (and Mayor of Dallas) Eric Johnson. Texas State Bill HB1629,[3] addressing crowdfunding portals for small business, is a direct result of his staff's attendance at a Black Chamber of Commerce (TAAACC) conference.[4]

Joining a Chamber is a way to become knowledgeable about and participate in public policy discussion that may directly impact your business.

Another benefit is *promotion*. Many Chambers have member databases that are distributed to large corporations, state and local government agencies, and news organizations. Especially for those just starting out, Chambers are an easy way to let the world know you are open for business.

Discounts and other benefits. Many Chambers offer discounts on business services, like insurance, health care plans, and office supplies. While most of these discounts are not large enough to justify membership on their own, they are a nice add-on.

Most Chambers charge an annual membership fee. Some of these are significant, so to determine the worth of the membership organization, consider the following:

---

[3] https://capitol.texas.gov/BillLookup/History.aspx?LegSess=84R&Bill=HB1629
[4] Dallas Weekly Newspaper. August 18, 2015. www.creativeinvest.com/TexasEconomic ForecastCrowdfundingBill.pdf

1. As we have stated throughout this book, we suggest moving away from a selfish, what's-in-it-for-me, money-only focus. Yes, it is important to use these organizations to help you make money, but given the crisis we face, opportunities for cooperation and collaboration are the more important considerations.

2. To determine if there are opportunities, attend a few meetings or webinars. In the current environment, most of these are free. After attending, carefully evaluate the relevance and quality of the meeting.

3. Reach out to organization members to get additional insight and information.

4. Sign up for the organization's email newsletter. Review their social media (Twitter, Facebook, Instagram, etc.) assets. Add to it: write a blog post, tweet, or Facebook post to let others know what your first impressions of the organization are.

5. Join a committee and participate.

■ **Note**   Use this listing at your own risk. While many of these organizations are legitimate, some may not be. Most have not been verified and validated by the author.

Summary Count of Ethnic Chambers and Other Organizations in the United States

To obtain insight, we created a database listing Asian, Black, and Hispanic Chambers of Commerce and other minority business groups. There are 481 organizations in total, with 304 being focused on the Asian or East Indian community, 68 Black Chambers or other business networking organizations, and 109 Hispanic organizations. Obviously, the actual number of organizations serving these groups far exceeds our tally here, but we wanted to provide general information. If you want more detail, you can download the data from our website.

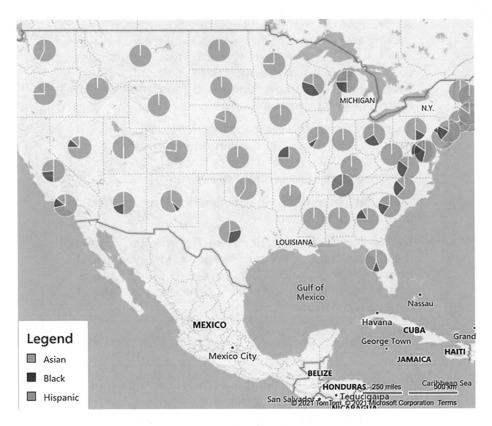

Map showing Chambers of Commerce and other organizations, by state, ethnic group. Gold = Black, blue = Asian, purple = Hispanic

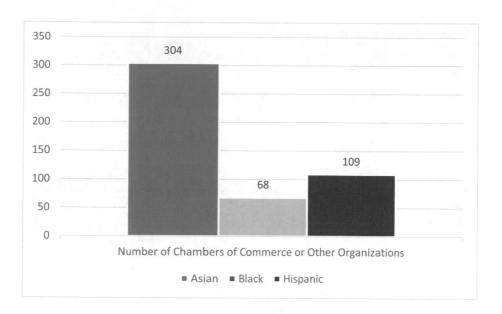

Black Chambers of Commerce

The following table shows our count of Black Chambers of Commerce by state. As we noted, the list is not a fully verified, but rather a quick data review. We have provided a link to the list on our website: www. creativeinvest.com.

Count: Black Chamber by State (Estd.)

State	Number	State	Number	State	Number	State	Number
AZ	2	LA	1	NM	1	SC	1
CA	18	MD	4	NV	1	TN	1
DC	3	MI	2	NY	5	TX	10
FL	3	MO	1	OH	3	VA	2
GA	2	NC	2	PA	1	WI	2
IL	1	NJ	1	RI	1	Total	68

Hispanic Chambers of Commerce

The following table lists our count of Hispanic Chambers of Commerce, by state. As we noted, the data is not a fully verified, but rather a quick review. As with our list of Black Chambers, we provide a link to the list on entities on our website: www.creativeinvest.com.

Count: Hispanic Chambers by State

State	Number	State	Number	State	Number	State	Number
AR	1	IL	4	NJ	1	RI	1
AZ	3	LA	1	NM	8	SC	1
CA	21	MA	2	NV	1	TN	2
CO	3	MD	2	NY	4	TX	15
CT	2	MI	2	OH	4	UT	1
DC	2	MN	1	OK	2	VA	1
FL	13	NC	1	OR	1	WA	3
GA	1	NE	1	PA	3	WI	1
						Total	109

Asian Chambers of Commerce and Other Organizations

The following table shows our count of Asian Chambers of Commerce and other organizations, by state. As we noted, the list is not a fully verified, but rather a quick data review. As with our list of Black and Hispanic Chambers, we provide a link to the list on our website: www.creativeinvest.com.

Count: Asian Chambers, Orgs by State

State	Number	State	Number	State	Number	State	Number
AK	5	IL	7	NC	5	SC	3
AL	13	IN	5	ND	4	SD	3
AZ	5	KS	5	NE	4	TN	4
CA	39	KY	5	NH	5	TX	7
CO	10	LA	5	NJ	11	UT	1
CT	5	MA	11	NM	5	VA	4
DC	11	MD	7	NV	6	VT	4
DE	5	ME	3	NY	14	WA	4
FL	13	MI	4	OH	5	WI	2
GA	9	MN	3	OK	3	WV	1
HI	8	MO	3	OR	3	WY	2
IA	5	MS	3	PA	2	Total	304
ID	6	MT	3	RI	4		

International Chambers of Commerce

Some of the oldest Chambers of Commerce in the world are outside of the United States. These include the following:

The International Chamber of Commerce, established in 1919, boasts a membership of "hundreds of thousands of member companies from more than 130 countries." https://iccwbo.org/

Formed in 1927, the Federation of Indian Chambers of Commerce and Industries (FICCI) "is the largest and oldest apex business organisation in India." The organization claims 300,000 direct and indirect members. www.ficci.in/index.asp

There are dozens of similar organizations around the world (see www.entrepreneur.com/article/40332). If your business is international in nature, these organizations may be useful. If you are purely domestic, less so. Overall, the utility of these organizations will vary significantly, depending on the time you have to devote to the organization, as with all other membership groups.

Corporate Supplier Diversity Organizations

Corporate supplier diversity programs are formal efforts to increase the number, type, and breadth of minority- and women-owned firms supplying goods and services to large corporations. One of the first supplier diversity programs was created as a result of urban unrest in the 1960s and was started by General Motors.[5] As we discussed in an earlier chapter, an amendment to the law that created the Small Business Administration (SBA), Public Law 95-507, encouraged government contractors to utilize minority-owned businesses.

■ **Supplier Diversity**   A supplier diversity program is a private or government sector initiative that develops policies, practices, and procedures to encourage the use of women- and minority-owned firms in the provision of goods and services.

The focus on corporate spending led to the creation of several organizations designed to facilitate and help corporations find and use minority firms. While some of these organizations are useful, many are not. The issue is the gatekeeper role that these supplier diversity groups play.

They, as a singular part of their mission, certify, evaluate, and, as a result, limit the ability of minority firms to do business with large corporations.

Despite the gatekeepers, it is still possible for minority- and women-owned businesses to gain access to and do business with large corporations. But this requires a direct approach.

In 2009, I provided to Pacific Gas and Electric Company (PG&E) social and financial credit ratings covering commercial banks serving areas of high social need within PG&E's service territory.[6] Using our ratings, PG&E made FDIC-insured deposits in 15 banks, including minority- and community-based institutions. I gained PG&E as a client without any of the typical minority business certifications, by directly appealing to the firm's treasurer.

Figure 5-3 shows the result of our direct approach. The portfolio we constructed for Pacific Gas and Electric yielded 1.26%. Alternative investments were yielding 0.18%, 0.31%, and 0.98%.

---

[5] Why You Need a Supplier-Diversity Program, HBR August 17, 2020, https://hbr.org/2020/08/why-you-need-a-supplier-diversity-program
[6] Creative Investment studies community development and minority-owned financial institutions for PG&E. April 27, 2009. For a full description of the PG&E project, see www.impactinvesting.online/2009/04/creative-investment-studies-community.html

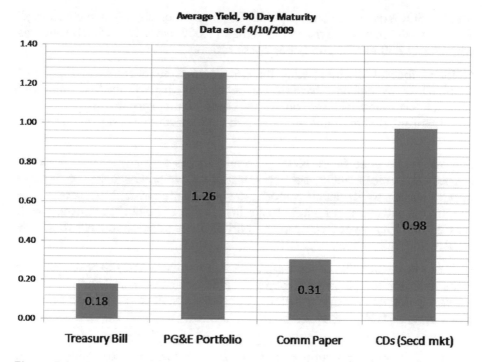

Figure 5-3. Result of the PG&E Project

Fortunately, social media platforms like LinkedIn and Facebook make it much easier to reach corporate decision-makers. We think this is a key strategy that you must use effectively in order to uncover significant opportunities. While we will discuss these strategies in a later chapter, it is important to note that there are LinkedIn marketing tools available for every business size and type, from small to large and B2B to B2C. Spend time getting to know these tools. Specialized services and consultants can help you. Consider spending time and money to effectively understand, and use, these resources.

National Minority Supplier Development Council Inc (NMSDC)

The growth of women and minority businesses has given rise to a number of distinct, separate organizations focused on this sector. These include the following:

NMSDC: The National Minority Supplier Development Council Inc (NMSDC) provides services to corporations and helps with corporate supplier diversity programs. NMSDC also certifies women- and minority-owned firms.

The NMSDC structure consists of "23 Regional Councils across the country." The Councils "certify and match more than 12,000 minority-owned businesses with over 1,450 NMSDC member corporations."

NMSDC focuses on integrating minority-owned suppliers into the global supply diversity pipeline, based on a belief that this will lead to improved "market share and reduced operating costs" for corporate members. We found similar benefits when we researched the impact of diversity on corporate profits (see www.diversityfund.net).

For minority-owned firms, NMSDC offers access to many of the country's largest and most influential corporations. NMSDC seeks to create opportunities to connect minority-owned firms with their corporate supporters and members. These larger firms want to "build relationships with trusted minority-owned companies." NMSDC has positioned itself to supply "trusted" minority suppliers.

One of the key benefits of this organization is its reach. They expose minority firms to major companies that may be hidden or not very well known. This is especially important now, as major corporations seek to make good on their Black Lives Matter pledges.

We worked with NMSDC member firm Foodbuy, LLC, the foodservice industry's leading procurement services organization, to address the economics of diversity with their organization. We developed the IMM framework for this discussion: Innovation, Money, and Momentum, described in Figure 5-4.

Figure 5-4. From Foodbuy "Diversity Matters" Talk and Session. October 2020

While we were aware of Foodbuy's parent company, Compass Group, we were not aware of Foodbuy itself and the fact that the firm "negotiates and contracts for more than $20bn of food, beverages, and services."

This is an example of the exposure and the benefit NMSDC can provide. See https://nmsdc.org/nmsdc-regional-affiliates-list/ for more.

Global Supplier Diversity Alliance

A global network of supplier diversity advocates covering five countries. These organizations are focused on providing opportunities for women- and minority-owned firms globally.[7] These advocacy organizations are

- Australia: Supply Nation – "Supply Nation provides Australia's leading database of verified Indigenous businesses: search by business name, product, service, area, or category." https://supplynation.org.au/

- Canada: Canadian Aboriginal and Minority Supplier Council (CAMSC) – "CAMSC's Mission – To champion business relationships and economic growth of the Canadian supply chain through the inclusion of Aboriginals and Minority suppliers." www.camsc.ca/

- China: Minority Supplier Development in China (MSDChina) – "Minority Supplier Development in China (MSD China) focuses on minority supplier development, which is a facet of supplier diversity. Supplier diversity is a relatively new concept in China. As a result, a lot of entrepreneurs, government officers and procurement executives don't necessarily know what it is."

- South Africa: South African Supplier Diversity Council (SASDC) – "The primary goal of the SASDC is to promote supplier diversity by encouraging, supporting and assisting its member corporations to open up business opportunities and progressively increase the transaction with certified black-owned businesses. Participation by black-owned companies in South Africa's corporate of supply chains remains alarmingly low." www.sasdc.org.za/

---

[7] "Entrepreneurs from ethnic minorities face an uneven playing field in the U.K.: Half of White business owners meet their financial aims, well ahead of 30% for Black entrepreneurs, a new study finds." Bloomberg. October 21, 2020. www.bloomberg.com/news/articles/2020-10-21/bame-entrepreneurs-face-systemic-disadvantage-in-u-k

- UK: Minority Supplier Development UK (MSDUK) – "MSDUK is proud to champion the best of British Ethnic Minority Businesses and work with progressive global corporations that understand the value of supply chain inclusion and diversity." www.msduk.org.uk/about-us/

Money: Digital Payment Services, Credit, Banks, Venture Capital, and Other Resources

How to Get Money for Your Minority Business

W. M. Cunningham, *Thriving As a Minority-Owned Business in Corporate America*,
https://doi.org/10.1007/978-1-4842-7240-4_6

Money is a major factor in minority business development, but it is not the only factor. Minority- and women-owned firms have survived without money, instead relying on creative persistence to succeed.

There are a number of new tools you can use to survive. These include alternative payment resources, like Bitcoin, Cash App, Venmo, and PayPal We have included selected slides from our free class on Udemy, How to Finance a Black Women-owned Business in 2021. `https://www.udemy.com/course/blackwomenbusinessfinancing/`.

Still, in order to really grow, there is no denying the need for conventional financial resources. Minority- and women-owned firms are experts at making the most with limited resources.

New Tools

In response to advances in the growth and use of digital networks, several payment tools have been developed that you can use to facilitate the flow of revenue. We believe you can use these tools to help reduce the impact of the lack of fairness in the banking and financial services marketplace.

The following table summarizes digital payment services:

Payment System	Description	Initial release date:	Operating system:	Website:	Owner	Customer Service Phone Number
Android Pay	Digital wallet and online payment system.	2015	Android, iOS (US)	https://pay.google.com/about/	Google	1-888-986-7944
Apple Pay	Mobile payment and digital wallet service. Allows users to make payments in person, in iOS apps, and on the web	2014	iPhone, Apple Watch, iPad, and Mac.	https://www.apple.com/apple-pay/	Apple	

Bitcoin	Digital currency.	2008	All, but must use an intermediary wallet program to link to a conventional bank account	https://bitcoin.org/en/	Public network	
CashApp	Mobile payment service allowing users to transfer money via a mobile phone app.	2013	Android, iOS	https://cash.app/	Square	1-855-351-2274
PayPal	Worldwide online payment system.	1998	Android, iOS	https://www.paypal.com/	PayPal Holdings, Inc.	1 (888) 221-1161
Square	Merchant services and mobile payment system.	2009	Android, iOS	https://squareup.com/us/en		1 (855) 700-6000
Venmo	Mobile payment service. Account holders transfer funds via a mobile phone app. Sender and receiver must be in the U.S.	2009	Android, iOS	https://venmo.com/	PayPal	1 (855) 812-4430

| Zelle | Digital payment network. | 2017 | Android, iOS | https://www.zellepay.com/ | Early Warning Services, owned by Bank of America, BB&T, Capital One, JPMorgan Chase, PNC Bank, U.S. Bank and Wells Fargo. | 1 (844) 428-8542 |

These payment systems offer a way that minority- and women-owned firms can overcome some of the obstacles that result from racial and gender discrimination in the provision of financial services. While they allow you to set up shop quickly and easily, they are not a panacea. You still need a conventional bank account, but at some point this will not be the case.

Why Minority and Women Firms Should Use Bitcoin

Bitcoin is the main form of digital money, or *cryptocurrency*.

A cryptocurrency is a digital program or asset designed to work like currency.[1] This is money purely in digital form. It is not tied to gold, oil, or paper money, although its value is established by reference to these assets. Some digital money, like bitcoin, are infinitely divisible. You can buy $1 worth of bitcoin or $1 million.

Bitcoin highlights the hidden, fourth function of money. The three widely recognized main functions of money are as a medium of exchange, a unit of account, and a store of value. There is a fourth function of money that is hidden and rarely discussed: *as a means of social control*.

---

[1] See www.impactinvesting.online/2017/05/summary-of-bitcoin-and-its-underlying.html

Bitcoin moved above $15,000 in early November 2020. In April 2021, it reached $64,899. As a business financing tool (invest a small dollar amount and see it grow over a very short period of time), bitcoin literally has no peer. There is no, and I mean NO, reason to believe this phenomenal price growth will continue. There are other reasons to be aware of this new tool, however.

I've been suggesting that minority- and women-owned firms use bitcoin for some time. In October 2019, I advised placing a small dollar amount ($100) into bitcoin as a way of exploring its utility during my 2016, 2017, 2018, and 2020 Economic Forecast to the Texas Association of African American Chambers of Commerce.

At some point, minority- and women-owned firms will be able to implement transactions using this currency: if someone wants $1 worth of your goods or services, you could sell them your product via digital currency. You give them the product, and they transfer $1 worth of bitcoin to your digital wallet. This occurs without going through the existing banking system, which we know is hostile to minority and specifically African American firms.

For more, see the following:

Free Class: Bitcoin and Blockchain Explained IN 30 MINUTES: Understanding Bitcoin and Blockchain. www.udemy.com/course/bitcoin-explained/

Summary of bitcoin and its underlying technology. www.impactinvesting. online/2017/05/summary-of-bitcoin-and-its-underlying.html

Blockchain 1.0. www.impactinvesting.online/2017/05/blockchain-10.html

Blockchain, Cryptocurrency and the Future of Monetary Policy. www.prlog. org/12785779-blockchain-cryptocurrency-and-the-future-of-monetary-policy.html

Creative Investment Research Files Comment on FedNow Payment System. www.prlog.org/12791364-creative-investment-research-files-comment-on-fednow-payment-system.html

Is FedCoin, a US Government-issued cryptocurrency, feasible? www.prlog. org/12772509-is-fedcoin-us-government-issued-cryptocurrency-feasible.html

Comments to the Reserve Bank of India on Blockchain, Crypto. www.prlog. org/12765825-comments-to-the-reserve-bank-of-india-on-blockchain-crypto.html

Cash App

Square Cash allows customers to pay you via Cash App. The product does not allow you to manage any employees who are taking payments for you, monitor inventory, or generate reports. You get a username, a "cashtag," that customers use to pay your business. Given these factors, this tool is suited for single-person firms, or sole proprietors, and we note that most African American businesses are sole proprietors.

Customers can also pay by going to your payment page, a custom URL. You can post the link to your website, without having to have an account. Fees are 2.75% per transaction. Transfers will cost you 1.5%. If your business processes $20,000 during a given year, you will be required to file an IRS 1099-K form.[2]

Individuals are the focus of Cash App accounts, but you can set up your account for a business by changing the account type to business. You can reverse this designation if you need to.

PayPal

PayPal is probably the best way minority- and women-owned firms can accept credit card payments. Firms can accept credit card payments on a website or on a third-party online marketplace like eBay or Etsy. Customers do not need to set up a PayPal account to send you money via credit card.

Business Loans

PayPal also offers a **Business Loan program**:

- The Program offers loans from $5000 to $500,000.

- It is best suited for businesses with at least nine months in business and $42,000+ in annual revenue. A PayPal Business account is required to fund your loan (processing payments with PayPal is optional).

- The loan is a fixed-term loan that is automatically repaid out of your PayPal or business banking account on a weekly basis.

- Funding time – Funding in as fast as the next business day.

- Credit check – Checking eligibility will not affect your credit score.

---

[2]www.national.biz/how-use-cash-app-your-business-complete-guide/

www.paypal.com/webapps/mpp/paypal-business-loan

PayPal Working Capital Loan Program

According to Investopedia, "Working capital is the difference between a company's current assets, such as cash, accounts receivable (customers' unpaid bills) and inventories of raw materials and finished goods, and its current liabilities, such as accounts payable."

PayPal's Working Capital Loan program offers loans from $1000 to $125,000. The program is based on the amount of money that you process through your PayPal account. The loan is based on your PayPal sales history and is repaid out of your PayPal sales. You need to be an existing PayPal customer with a PayPal Business account for at least 90 days that has processed $15,000+ with PayPal within the last 12 months. The application itself is very straightforward. Approval and funding take minutes. Given the credit issues that minority and women firms have, it is nice to know that using this program does not affect your business or personal credit scores.

www.paypal.com/workingcapital/

Square

Square is a credit card and point-of-sale payment processor using mobile technology to allow you to accept card payments using a credit card reader, smartphone, or tablet.

Square offers perhaps the best way for your business to accept credit card payments.

https://squareup.com/us/en/square-one/business-management-tools

Venmo

Venmo, owned by PayPal, is a mobile payment app for Android and iOS devices. Since it is a social payment platform, Venmo has the added advantage of promoting a firm to a group of people, especially relevant for minority- and women-owned companies, especially those that target a specific ethnic group. Of course, the benefit received depends upon the products and services you offer, but the added functionality the system provides to your payment systems by allowing customers to split payments with their friends is important.

https://venmo.com/

Zelle

Zelle is a mobile payment application, developed by over 30 major US banks. It is a direct response to platforms like Venmo. Zelle is tightly integrated with mobile banking apps provided by major participating banks.

As one more way to get paid, Zelle is a solid option. Keep in mind that the historical discrimination banks have visited upon minority and women is likely to be embedded in this platform.

Business Credit Scores

If you are going to apply for business credit via any of the sources listed in the next section, you will benefit by checking your personal and business credit scores first. As with every other factor, you should understand that the same discriminatory practices that impact minority and women firms in lending and credit are present here as well. Still, reviewing this data for your firm is a must.

NAV

Start here: NAV provides both business and personal credit reports, operating under a freemium business model. This means they have a free service, but to get anything truly useful, you will have to pay to upgrade the service. Taking advantage of the fact that the site has both your personal and business credit history, NAV provides a list of suggested credit providers, including some of those listed in the "Business Loan Resources" section.

www.nav.com/

Dun & Bradstreet PAYDEX

PAYDEX is a business credit scoring system developed by Dun & Bradstreet (D&B). The system reviews data on business payment performance, that is, it reviews how promptly a business pays its bills. The PAYDEX score is the business equivalent of an individual's FICO score.

https://businesscredit.dnb.com/

Experian Intelliscore Plus

It attempts to measure the business delinquency risk.

www.experian.com/business-information/credit-risk-management

FICO LiquidCredit Small Business Scoring Service

The FICO SBSS score, ranging from 0 to 300, is used to determine a business's eligibility for financing. The SBSS score combines a business owner's personal credit history with the business's credit profile.

www.fico.com/en/products/fico-small-business-scoring-service

Business Loan Resources

As with the payment platforms listed earlier, there has been a corresponding increase in the number and type of business lending resources. Many of these are relevant to minority and women businesses. The cost of these services is high, in some cases as high as 99%. These are usurious rates that make it harder for a small business to survive. You are, in essence, working for the lender. Still, in an emergency, and given the history of discrimination against minority- and women-owned firms, you may have limited choices.

Fundbox

Fundbox is a revolving line of credit lender. A revolving line of credit is a loan product that offers a predetermined amount of always available financing to an individual or corporation. The source of the financing is either a bank or a supplier/merchant. Typically, it is available continuously. The loan is considered a debt that is repaid periodically and can be used repeatedly once repaid. According to the website, "Fundbox makes capital available to businesses through business loans and lines of credit made by First Electronic Bank, a Utah chartered Industrial Bank, member FDIC, in addition to invoice-clearing advances, business loans and lines of credit made directly by Fundbox."

https://fundbox.com/

LoanBuilder

LoanBuilder, owned by PayPal, issues 13- to 52-week loans through WebBank, an FDIC-regulated bank.

www.loanbuilder.com/

www.webbank.com/

OnDeck

OnDeck provides up to $500,000 in business credit to small businesses. Borrower credit requirements are higher than with other providers.

www.ondeck.com/

Kabbage

Kabbage Funding provides borrowers from $2000 to $250,000 via a line of credit. The term of the loan ranges from 6, 12, or 18 months. Note that the actual installment loan is issued by Celtic Bank, a Utah-chartered FDIC-insured industrial bank. Also note that American Express recently acquired Kabbage.

www.kabbage.com/

Loan Resource Summary

The following table summarizes the preceding information.

Lending Resources			
FundBox			
Maximum Loan Amount	$100,000	**Payment Frequency**	Weekly
Minimum Credit Score	500	**Repayment Term**	6 months
Starting APR	Varies	**Funding Speed**	Next day
LoanBuilder			
Maximum Loan Amount	$500,000	**Payment Frequency**	Weekly
Minimum Credit Score	550	**Repayment Term**	12 months
Starting APR	Varies	**Funding Speed**	Next day
OnDeck			
Maximum Loan Amount	$500,000	**Payment Frequency**	Weekly
Minimum Credit Score	600	**Repayment Term**	36 months
Starting APR	Varies	**Funding Speed**	Next day
Kabbage			
Maximum Loan Amount	$250,000	**Payment Frequency**	Weekly
Minimum Credit Score	560	**Repayment Term**	18 months
Starting APR	Varies	**Funding Speed**	Next day

Banks

Years ago, banks were the primary source of small business credit. They aren't anymore. Banks have been pushed out of their primary role in this marketplace by credit unions, online lenders, payday lenders, and cryptocurrency. According to the National Small Business Association, "small business bank loans totaled nearly $600 billion in 2015. At the same time, lending from alternative sources such as finance companies and peer-to-peer, or P2P, marketplace lenders amounted to $593 billion."

Most startup small businesses "rely on the personal savings of the founders and their family. In 2015, startups relied on bank loans 8% and business credit cards 2% of the time. And while 57% of small businesses did not expand, 22% expanded with personal and family savings, while venture and angel capital accounted for less than 2% of financing."[3]

For minority- and women-owned firms, banks are an unreliable source of financing. This is confirmed by recent studies. In 2014, three "business school professors decided to hold an experiment: they sent a group of Caucasian, African-American, and Hispanic entrepreneurs to banks to inquire small business loans. They even dressed them in matching outfits." The results were clear:

> White business owners got better and more encouraging service … Bank employees were more likely to tell them about loan terms and fees and more likely to offer help filling out an application. Bankers were more likely to ask minority entrepreneurs about their personal finances and less likely to offer the black and Hispanic mystery shoppers a business card.

Maturity of the Loan

Time to maturity, or the length of the loan contract. Loans can be short term (less than one year), intermediate term (one to five years), and long term (greater than five years). Note that "revolving credit and perpetual debt have no fixed date for retirement. Banks provide revolving credit through extension of a line of credit." This is still considered a loan.

Dollar Amount

The amount of the loan typically reflects both the needs of the business and the amount the financial institution is able to lend, given the social factors noted earlier. Loan amounts granted by a financial institution can be independent of the dollar amount requested. According to the latest data

---

[3] www.sba.gov/sites/default/files/Finance-FAQ-2016_WEB.pdf

from the Federal Reserve, the average small business loan amount in 2019 is $633,000 in the United States, and according to the US Department of Commerce, the average loan received by high sales minority firms was $363,000 compared with $592,000 for nonminority firms.

Deciding How Long You Need to Borrow the Funds For

In general, you should borrow money for the longest time period you can at the lowest interest rate you can find.

Eligibility Criteria for Bank Loans

Bank loans are hard to get. According to the NSBA report, only 15% of small businesses received a loan through a large bank. Interest rates for business loans from large banks, in general, are around 4% to 10%. Terms also vary, but banks tend to provide long-term financing with manageable monthly payments.

With bank loans, your eligibility depends on a number of factors: Are you taking out a personal loan? Do you have any assets that can be used to secure the loan? How long have you been in business? Are you a woman or minority? Where are you (and the business) located? A personal loan has eligibility criteria that differ from those for a business loan. The length of the loan term is also a factor. If you just want an overnight loan, as opposed to a 30-year loan, the risk that the bank will not be repaid falls, and so does the eligibility criteria. Other eligibility factors for personal loans relate to employment, loan security, assets, debts and expenses, and your credit history.

Personal loans link to your credit as an individual and have rules that differ slightly from business loan requirements. You generally need a credit score that exceeds 550. (Order a free credit report once a year on AnnualCreditReport.com. See our section on credit scores on the credit cards page). Even if you have bad credit, you can apply for a business loan using your personal credit information. Just be aware that the chances of approval go down, of course. You may have the option of a secured personal loan, but it's less likely that you'll need to provide collateral with a personal loan than with a business loan.

Income

Most lenders require that you have a steady income, to help guarantee that you can make the minimum monthly payments as set by the loan contract.

Employment

You need to be employed on a full-time basis for most personal small business loans. You should note that if you're employed part-time or are self-employed, there are still loan options. And also note that even if you're unemployed, there are lenders who accept government benefits as a form of income, but these are few. Interest rates will be higher as well.

Loan Security

A secured loan uses an asset (car, house) as guarantee of repayment. With an unsecured loan, your credit score is the main factor used to determine if you get the loan.

Documentation

The following documents are required along with your business or personal loan application:

- Personal credit score — The lender will access this information from one or more of the three different personal credit bureaus: Equifax, TransUnion, or Experian.

- Business credit score — Credit use, credit history, business credit card payments, the size of your company, risk factors in your industry. There are also different firms, like Dun & Bradstreet, that measure business credit.

- Basic personal information — Your name (or any other name you've ever used), address, SSN, valid ID, etc.

- Basic business information and permits — Business operating address, entity type, and employer identification number (EIN).

Benefits of bank loans to the borrower

- If you can get a loan, banks tend to offer favorable terms.

- Pay only the principal and interest amount on a loan. No ownership dilution.

- Interest paid on the loan may be tax-deductible.

- Borrower chooses the length of the loan and amount.

Minority-Owned Banks

To counter the discrimination documented earlier, many have pointed to banks owned by members of affected minority groups as a source of business financing. While this might appear to be a reasonable response, the facts show that the impact and effectiveness of these banks varies widely. Factors that influence this performance include the nature of the minority group cited.

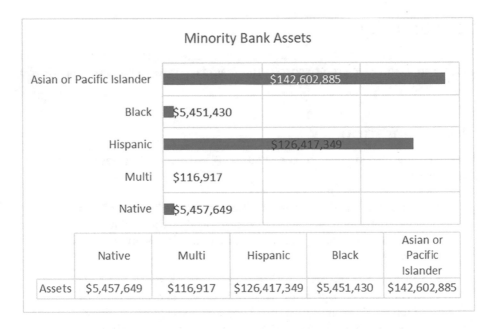

Minority Bank Assets

	Native	Multi	Hispanic	Black	Asian or Pacific Islander
Assets	$5,457,649	$116,917	$126,417,349	$5,451,430	$142,602,885

With $126 billion and $142 billion in assets, respectively, Hispanic and Asian-owned banks are much more effective facilitators of small business financing for members of their ethnic groups than African American banks, the latter being too small ($5 billion in assets, or 1.8% of the assets held by Hispanic and Asian banks) and few in number to have meaningful impact. Total US Bank Assets were $21 trillion in the second quarter of 2020.

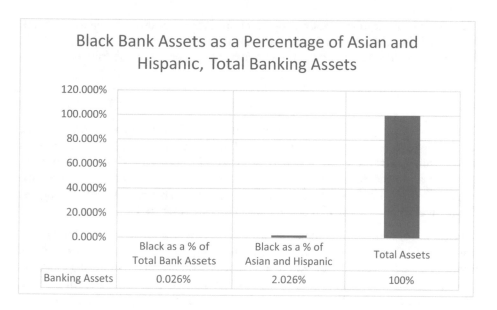

Black Bank Assets as a Percentage of Asian and Hispanic, Total Banking Assets			
	Black as a % of Total Bank Assets	Black as a % of Asian and Hispanic	Total Assets
Banking Assets	0.026%	2.026%	100%

As with all of the factors outlined in this book, understand that if you have business or personal connections (or significant contacts) with Black banks, you may be able to get a loan. Otherwise, we would not count on this source.

The FDIC site has lists of minority banks in the United States.

www.fdic.gov/regulations/resources/minority/mdi.html

Venture Capital

Ahhh, venture capital, the quaint and entirely American notion that if you send some stranger a business plan, they will send you a million dollars. We wouldn't bet on it if you are a woman- or minority-owned company.

Most, but not all, venture capital firms and government financing programs targeting minorities and, to a lesser extent, women are ineffective. This includes the SBA.[4]

In addition to the problems with discrimination, venture capital was simply not designed for the current situation, with a 41% decline in Black businesses and a massive decline in GDP. Even with the recent push to "diversify" venture capital, we do not think this source of capital effective. We have included, in the appendix, a response we received from one Black women run "VC" firm

---

[4] The Paycheck Protection Program failed many Black-owned businesses, www.vox.com/2020/10/5/21427881/paycheck-protection-program-black-owned-businesses?utm_campaign=vox&utm_content=entry&utm_medium=social&utm_source=twitter via @voxdotcom.

concerning an inquiry about a product initiative to save the lives of Black women. Still, given the fascination and obsession with venture capital, we have included an evaluation and targeted information resources as follows.

Basics

Venture capital (VC) firms invest in startup and early-stage firms. Venture capital investments usually start at $250,000 and are mainly in "businesses that exhibit extremely high growth potential." If they invest, these firms expect to earn a significant return on their investment. For example, one venture capital firm, in 1996, invested $2 million in Lycos, an Internet search engine. That investment was worth $427 million at the start of 1999.

Another VC firm told a small minority company we know that "Unless you foresee revenues in the ballpark of $20 million in year 3 for the product this would not be a venture target. Thank you so much for considering BLANK Venture Partners." If your venture does not have a chance of meeting these investment return and revenue targets, reconsider seeking venture capital.

Venture capital firms are also discriminatory.[5] The majority of women- and minority-owned firms (and nonminority firms, for that matter) will never receive an investment from *any* venture capital firm.

They depend, however, on your ideas.

Most venture capital firms cannot correctly evaluate investment opportunities in minority markets. They don't have the personnel or the desire to do so. Still, if you feel your business will, in fact, generate "revenues in the ballpark of $20 million in year 3 for the product," give them a shot.

But, be careful. Before you send them anything to any venture capital firm, get a signed confidentiality agreement. Or, send a stripped down version of your business plan, without all of the secrets. Many VC firms simply collect good business plans and ideas, which they then develop. We feel this will be especially problematic for minority firms.

Prospects for minority- and women-owned firms seeking funding: Poor. A VC firm may see 1000 business plans in a year and only fund 10. You do the math. Your chances with these firms are, in essence, zero.

For more, see Small Business Financing, Black People and Venture Capital, https://youtu.be/gXGBEUoxHHs via @YouTube.

---

[5] Bias and Discrimination in Fundraising, www.holloway.com/g/venture-capital/sections/bias-and-discrimination-in-fundraising via @holloway.

You can view a list of Black Women at

www.crunchbase.com/lists/black-women-in-vc/35fe0366-ad51-4402-b472-ef6a1762c381/identifiers

Source: Crunchbase. Black Women in VC.

Accelerators

In 1954, my father, Paul Nicholas Cunningham, formed a collaborative entity consisting of recent graduates from the School of Architecture at Howard University. They shared office space and supported each other. I replicated this approach with the formation of a Black business collaborative house at the WeWork Wonder Bread location, two blocks away from Howard.

Minority businesses have often used collaborative approaches to support each other. These have included cooperative and collaborative entities that resemble accelerators.

Modern-day accelerators are used to support venture capital investments. These tend to be a facility and fund created to identify and assist newly created firms.

While we think these may be useful for minority firms, the unrelenting focus on money and the greed it exposes are wrong for minority firms. We think a more collaborative approach is the way to go.

Still, because of their ubiquity, they may be a way to supercharge your start. We have listed several of these facilities as follows.

Startup accelerator programs in the United States, http://brook.gs/2bd7NHt via @BrookingsInst

	Incubators	Angel investors	Accelerators	Hybrid
Duration	1 to 5 years	Ongoing	3 to 6 months	3 months to 2 years
Cohorts	No	No	Yes	No
Business model	Rent; non-profit	Investment	Investment; can also be non-profit	Investment; can also be non-profit
Selection	Non-competitive	Competitive, ongoing	Competitive, cyclical	Competitive, ongoing
Venture stage	Early or late	Early	Early	Early
Education	Ad hoc, human resources, legal	None	Seminars	Various incubator and accelerator practices
Mentorship	Minimal, tactical	As needed by investor	Intense, by self and others	Staff expert support, some mentoring
Venture location	On-site	Off-site	On-site	On-site

While there has been recent attention on accelerators for Black and minority firms,[6] these support and financing options are still heavily skewed to support white male–run firms.

We list here accelerators that have stated they are supportive of women.

Organization Name	Website
SheEO	https://sheeo.world/
Launch Tennessee	http://launchtn.org
Women's Startup Lab	http://womenstartuplab.com
JLABS	http://jlabs.jnjinnovation.com/
Monarq Incubator	https://www.monarqincubator.com/
Change Catalyst	http://changecatalyst.co/
The Refinery	http://therefineryct.com/accelerator
Equita	http://www.equita.co
WESST	http://www.wesst.org/
Mi Kitchen es su Kitchen	http://mikitchenessukitchen.com

---

[6]See https://drive.google.com/file/d/1NAdK23KpnRgBwVEKgjYKl2ZXCD6CWrrw/view?usp=sharing

EY Entrepreneurial Winning Women	http://www.ey.com/US/en/Services/Strategic-Growth-Markets/Entrepreneurial-Winning-Women
Y Combinator	http://www.ycombinator.com
500 Startups	http://500.co
NewMe Accelerator	http://www.newme.in/
AlphaLab	http://alphalab.org
Dreamit Ventures	http://www.dreamit.com
digitalundivided	http://www.digitalundivided.com
Start-Up Chile	http://startupchile.org
MergeLane	http://www.mergelane.com
The Brandery	http://brandery.org
Entrepreneurs Roundtable Accelerator	http://eranyc.com
Springboard Enterprises	http://www.sb.co
SMASHD Labs	http://smashdlabs.co/
Plug and Play Tech Centre	https://www.plugandplaytechcenter.com/
Prosper Women Entrepreneurs	http://www.prosperstl.com/
Women Founders Network	https://www.womenfoundersnetwork.com
Sephora Accelerate	http://www.sephorastands.com/accelerate/
DivInc	https://divinc.org/
XSquared Angels	https://www.rev1ventures.com/investments/x-squared-angels/
Hera Labs	http://www.hera-labs.com/
Female Founders Global	https://www.femalefounders.global/accelerator
AVINDĒ	http://avinde.org
Innovation Depot	http://innovationdepot.org/
Aviatra Accelerator	http://aviatraaccelerators.org/

The Big Push	http://www.thebigpush.ca
Female Founders Accelerator	http://femalefounders.hatchenterprise.org
The S Factory	http://www.thesfactory.org/index.html
Upstart Accelerator	http://upstartaccelerator.com/
Ready, Set, Raise	https://www.femalefounders.org/readysetraise
Women's Tech Accelerator by Brad Deals	http://www.bradsdeals.com/about-us/womens-tech-accelerator/
Her Future Accelerator	http://herfuturesummit.org/her-future-accelerator-launches-for-future-tech-female-pioneers-tackling-global-sdg-challenges/?fbclid=IwAR1gRbjBDI_9T8X8HI4z_vrzdxq1o9TbZUv4JxowS9ye51tg2dxRqVoRss8
La Cocina	https://lacocinasf.org/
SAP Foundries	https://sap.io/foundries/

New Perspectives from Black and Brown Entrepreneurs

Where We Are Now

2020 was a year of biblical proportions, with almost too many meaningful events to count. Among everything the year brought our way, one of the most positive has been Kamala Harris, the first female and person of color to become the Vice President of the United States. Harris epitomizes the best

© William Michael Cunningham 2021
W. M. Cunningham, *Thriving As a Minority-Owned Business in Corporate America*,
https://doi.org/10.1007/978-1-4842-7240-4_7

of a new, more diverse country–mixed race, born of immigrants, and a self-made success. From King to Obama to Harris, we have come a long way, but as consequential as they are, they represent only a fragment of the black and brown American experience.

Black and brown entrepreneurs have always been an economic force in America, in 2020 creating 4.7 million jobs and $700 billion in revenue. At the same time, they're too often the most negatively impacted by economic events. For example, at the start of 2020, we saw a 41% decline in black businesses, as a direct result of COVID-19 (Creative Investment Research). Although corporations pledged over $67 billion to support Black Lives Matter (BLM), the majority of these funds will be allocated slowly, through layers of bureaucracy, while the need to access funds has continued to grow.

Most modern polls, even those using sophisticated data algorithms, find it almost impossible to get an accurate picture of what's really happening with minority businesses. Collecting data via Prox, we met with a cross-section of small business owners, male and female, immigrant and non-immigrant, a writer, a fitness influencer, a business coach, and a professional soccer player, to name a few, to gain a realistic perspective into the current lives of black and brown entrepreneurs. What lessons can they share from their path to business ownership? What can we do to support them and other aspiring entrepreneurs?

The Results

The path to entrepreneurship. Becoming an entrepreneur was not by happenstance. Black and brown entrepreneurs chose the path to entrepreneurship out of pure motivation, drive, and passion and had a role model who helped to inspire their journey. At the same time, a little less than half took to entrepreneurship out of necessity.

Business ownership. Over half of the respondents owned more than one business and, despite current economic conditions, continue to see a level of profitability.

General challenges. Access to capital, resources, and mentorship remains to be the biggest challenge faced by black and brown entrepreneurs. Lending discrimination, customer discrimination, and community and family pushback persist, but remain isolated.

Impact of the pandemic. Even against all odds, half of our interviewees saw growth during the pandemic; however, the other half saw a negative impact due to shutdowns. And while major corporations seemed to benefit from government loans and grants during the pandemic, none of our black and brown businesses received any form of government support.

Black Lives Matter. While the BLM movement created more awareness and mainly had a positive impact, no one in our group received any direct investment or funding.

Their Advice for Other Entrepreneurs?

SBA, PTAC, and other organizations to network with and find ways of finding clients

- **Kellen Coleman**

It's ok not to have a blueprint that looks like other businesses to be successful. Many times, we are told it has to operate a certain way to be successful, and that's not true. We just need the right mentors and thought partners around us to help us both realize this and not get distracted by chasing a mission that isn't true to what our vision is.

- **Dynasti Hunt**

Find a mentor.

- **Tash Salas**

Stay focused, persistent, and consistent.

- **Sidney Rivera**

Work your network. A healthy network is filled with different types of people with different strengths. You must help each other and together you all rise.

- **Jeri Villarreal**

Make sure to read up before starting especially if you don't have a mentor. Don't be hesitant to ask other successful people that are in your field for advice.

- **Miriam Archibald**

Save your money and take strategic risks. There is never a right or a perfect time to start.

- **Djenane Fleurentin**

When you're watching everyone around you do the same work, and it's on par with your own, yet they're making more money than you, they are getting more clients or brand deals than you, you begin to wonder what it is you're doing wrong.

Suddenly, I realized the difference was pretty clear. I'd never really thought of myself as a minority before. I hadn't felt like I was treated much differently than my peers. However, while trying to build a business based on influence,

I began to feel that disparity. There will always be bias, but that doesn't mean you can't thrive. Sometimes, it means we have to work a little or a lot harder than others in order to break through, but you can, and you will break through.

— **Mercedes Moore**

Keep showing up. Even when you feel alone and unrepresented, and experience rejection over and over. Keep showing up. The more you show up for yourself, the more you pave the way for those who come after you. You might be a model for someone, just like those models I looked up to.

— **Kimberlee Morrison**

Spend quality time assessing your values, skills, talents, and vision. Make sure they are aligned before moving forward with your business.

— **Ronnie Witcher**

Learn how to communicate and how to influence people with integrity. Trust yourself and your talent. Cultivate a relentless pursuit of your goals and implementation of small action steps. Learn how to model, time blocking for outcomes, innovate, and measure. Never give up :)

— **Dayana Pereira**

Advice to Everyone: How You Can Help

Hire us, give us a try to get a new outlook on things.

— **Kellen Coleman**

Trust minority-owned businesses to do what they feel is best for their organization instead of providing funding that comes with a bunch of obligations and requirements that are necessary to meet. Unrestricted dollars that are provided are one of the best ways you can support an entrepreneur who is carving a new path instead of deciding for them what's best for them by restricting how they can use the funding you provide.

— **Dynasti Hunt**

Give them business and referrals :)

— **Tash Salas**

Look for causes that you care about and understand the business.

Sidney Rivera

Entrepreneurs may know that they need help but don't know what they need. Money is not always the answer and help needs to be very targeted and specific.

— **Jerri Villarreal**

Don't judge whether a minority business is worthy of your financial investment by its cover. Support more startups that have skin in the game.

— **Djenane Fleurentin**

It depends on the minority-owned party. For me, if someone were to ask me how they could help my business, the first thing I would say is to share my business. Help me reach more people who might be interested in my services. If they were interested in working with me personally, even better! I'm happy to discuss partnerships to get more reviews and testimonies to grow. As a group, listening, learning, and helping to educate.

— **Mercedes Moore**

Come to terms with your own implicit bias, and then do the work to dismantle that bias. For most of us, that's practicing a new level of self-awareness and checking our privilege on a daily basis. Then become intentional about using your own privilege to help underrepresented people in your industry.

— **Kimberlee Morrison**

Identify needs and root causes before providing what you "think" these entities need.

— **Ronnie Witcher**

Understand what the biggest challenges are. Listen first. See your future in them: support and monitor. Celebrate the wins. Keep building.

— **Dayana Pereira**

What Now?

Our Perspective

COVID reveals what's actually important: health, family, and community. It also shows what's not important: celebrity worship, money worship, and materialism. Globalization, too, a specific form of money worship, proved unable to support the domestic production of basic but critical supplies, like masks, in a time of crisis. Another fact revealed by this crisis is the true cost of racism. By limiting opportunity and competition, racism supports mediocrity.

These revelations call for a complete revisioning of the economy. Placing material gain above all else is simply wrong. A collaborative, cooperative economy focused on preserving and enhancing human life must now be the goal. As part of this effort, providing opportunities for people to lead meaningful, productive lives is primary. This is where supporting minority businesses come in. We are not saying that business is unimportant, but commercial activities serve life, not the other way around. Financial activities support business, not the reverse. This crisis shows how far out of alignment the culture has been. The focus on minority business helps readjust priorities.

The crisis reveals the moral and spiritual bankruptcy embedded in some of the major institutions in the country, materialistic and greed-based misinterpretations of the true goals of business. This is a self-centered version of "capitalism" that somehow justifies racial discrimination, to the detriment of the entire society, and business itself. In addition to being irrational, any logical interpretation reveals the selfishness driving this behavior. The common

© William Michael Cunningham 2021
W. M. Cunningham, *Thriving As a Minority-Owned Business in Corporate America*,
https://doi.org/10.1007/978-1-4842-7240-4_8

thread is veneration of white privilege, including the right to impose a deadly misallocation of resources on Black people, simply because some white people choose to do so. No appeal to free markets, personal liberty, or state's rights can justify the damage done to the entire community by irrational, undemocratic, antiscience-based behaviors. These mirror, directly, violent racial extremism.

Hatred of Black people, specifically the descendants of people who played a critical role in building the country, has always been prevalent. Blacks (not white women, Asians, Hispanics, or Native Americans) bore the brunt of the damage racism has caused and always knew this injury was going to metastasize. Targeting blacks is a reflection of white fear and mediocrity, nowhere better seen than in the performance of the former president. Another thing this crisis reveals is the central role falsification and lying play in white supremacy: in 1316 days, the former president told 22,247 lies.

Black people don't oppose white supremacy simply because it damages Black people. Historically, Blacks have tried to make the case that anti-Black racism imposes significant costs on the entire society. Those who promoted this line of reasoning have either been assassinated, like MLK, or assimilated, like Obama. Under either outcome, the result is the continuation of white supremacy to the now clear detriment of society. Both humanity and the planet continue to suffer.

Wealth Maximization Is the Wrong Goal

We suggest minority firms and individuals focus on life maximization, not wealth maximization. Why?

A materialistic focus will never be truly successful in a society that does everything it can to deny material comfort to Black people. The current assistance and attention minority and Black businesses are receiving is not new: we saw similar efforts in the months following the 1991 beating of Rodney King in LA. Eventually, this attention faded. While current attempts to help minority, specifically Black firms, may last longer than they did post Rodney King, this attention and assistance is sure to fade eventually. Racism is the water, not the shark.

The solution is to realize that wealth, in western culture at least, is a proxy for life. It is the tool that allows people to access resources (food, health care, water) that allows them to live.

Wealth and the Black Community

Wealth maximization is the wrong goal. Focus should be on
life maximization. Why?
A materialistic focus will never work in a society that does *everything it*
can to **deny material comfort to black people** as a way to
maximize white wealth.
Solution is to realize that wealth in this culture is a proxy for life.
In actuality, **wealth 👎 life.**
Black people are experts at survival and life maximization in a hostile
environment. THIS, not money, is your legacy.

BUT, in reality, wealth does not equal life: attempting to manipulate something that does not exist in reality is a waste of time. ("There is no spoon." From the movie *The Matrix*.) So, it is here.

Minorities, and Black people in particular, are experts at survival and life maximization in the most continually hostile environment on earth.

THIS, not money, is the way forward.

What Now for White People?

The path forward differs greatly depending upon what group and what assets you have access to. The suggestion for whites is as follows:

Hire Black people. Period. What Black people? Hire Black women. Why? Black women have the highest productivity and social impact. Racism and sexism impose heavy weights on most, yet, even in the face of these burdens, they have been able to make progress. Black women remain the driving force for social and economic justice in the United States.

Do business with minority firms. As noted in this book, minority firms suffer greatly in an economy that continually undervalues their worth. As with Black women, despite these burdens, many have succeeded greatly. This implies that, with adequate access to resources, these firms can do well. This book is about helping those firms do so.

Lower the return from racist behavior. Certain whites receive psychic income from racist behavior targeting African Americans. This psychic compensation lessens their need to maximize income in other ways, in the face of declining wages.

What Now for Black People?

For Black people, we suggest the following:

Assume we are never going back to "normal." We think the economy will never return to the position held prior to the pandemic.

Focus on the human, not the monetary. Focusing on human needs, not simply attempting to maximize profits, is the way forward. This almost certainly means that small business firms will make less money than they would otherwise. Some of this reduction in profit should be due to elevated costs related to supporting both employees (if you have any) and customers. We hope your firm provides goods and services that are considered essential. If you do, look for a way to lower the cost of your goods and services for your customers in the face of this crisis.

Cooperation, not competition. Black people need a truly collaborative and cooperative effort – in and by the Black community – a community often trained to be cutthroat to each other given the paucity of resources at its disposal. (After Creative Investment Research, in the public spirit, disseminated an estimate of corporate pledges to the Black Lives Matter cause (at $1.6 billion), several foundations made donations totaling $1.7 billion.) Now is the time to let go of negative and damaging habits for the survival of the Black community. In so doing, we will show the world the way out of the crisis.

Buy Bitcoin:

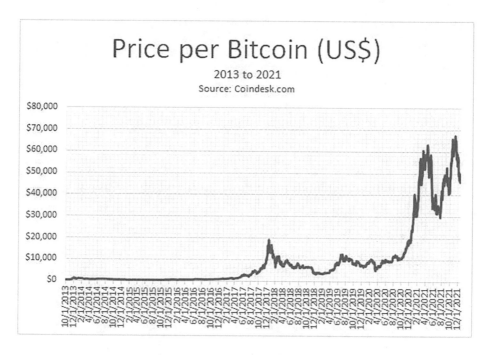

To maximize social and financial impact, in 2017, we suggested this strategy to several groups of Black women. See https://twitter.com/CreativeInv/status/1371995304417968128?s=20.

While you will note that the price of bitcoin has fallen from its high of $56,000 to $35,000 by June 12, 2021, this is of limited relevance, since a $10,000 purchase in 2017 would have been worth $600,000 by April of 2021 and $350,000 by June 2021, more than enough to finance a business.

Get a side hustle and apply for every grant, loan, etc. offered. We have a list of many of these resources on MinorityFinance.com. Please review the website, since this is a dynamic listing that changes frequently.

Corporate Pledges to Black Lives Matter

A Source of Capital?

The murder of George Floyd on May 25, 2020, sparked an immense global outcry for racial equity. Protests erupted across the world pleading for justice and the legitimization of the rights of Black people. Popularly referred to as the Black Lives Matter (BLM) movement, this outpouring of support dominated the American national conversation as millions of Americans demanded accountability and an end to racial injustice. BLM demonstrations took place in 4446 cities from May 25, 2020, to November 18, 2020. Protests in American cities to support Black Lives Matter occurred daily for weeks after the police killing of George Floyd. A perspective on the scope of the demonstrations has been provided by Alex Smith, a geographic information system analyst in Tucson, Arizona. His map can be found at www.creosotemaps.com/blm2020/.

(Contribute to the map by emailing creosotemaps@protonmail.com.)

© William Michael Cunningham 2021
W. M. Cunningham, *Thriving As a Minority-Owned Business in Corporate America*,
https://doi.org/10.1007/978-1-4842-7240-4_9

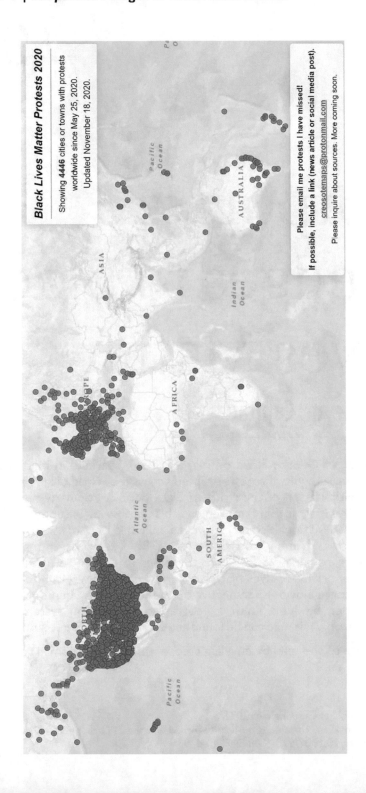

Black Lives Matter Protests 2020

Showing **4446** cities or towns with protests worldwide since May 25, 2020. Updated November 18, 2020.

Please email me protests I have missed!
If possible, include a link (news article or social media post).
creosotemaps@protonmail.com
Please inquire about sources. More coming soon.

Crucially, the private sector reacted at a level largely unseen and unheard of prior to Mr. Floyd's murder, as the vast majority of businesses posted messages of solidarity on social media. These entities sent employees and stakeholders messages and other communications in support of racial justice. Further, many made financial commitments to the Black community and organizations advocating racial equity. These pledges received great attention and praise, as corporations dug into their own treasuries to help the Black community.

Creative Investment Research was among the first to calculate and publish accurate, well-documented estimates for total BLM donations. We also were the first to compare these donations to donor net income. I have constructed a BLM Pledge Tracker, pictured as follows, to monitor activity in this sector.

Creative Investment Research

Corporate Donations to Black Lives Matter

May 15, 2020 - Aug 18, 2021

Corporate and Foundation Donation Summary. Confidential. Not for distribution or reproduction.   Copyright, 2020, WMC & Creative Investment Research

Number of Corporations

261

💲 N/A

0.0%

Amount Pledged

67,186,378,350

No data

2019 Fiscal Year Net Income

747,550,190,630

No data

Total Donated (Highest Level of Trust)

652,963,404

0.0%

Total Donated (Second Level of Trust)

1,892,176,000

0.0%

Total Combined

2,545,139,404

0.0%

Creative Investment Research 🏛

Number of Donations by Date

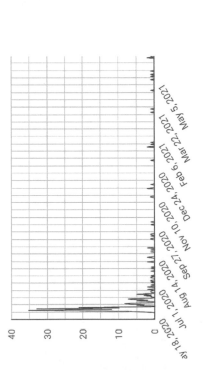

Corporate Donations by Date

	Name of Corporation	Date of Pledge ❷ ▾
1.	Google	Jun 17, 2021
2.	Apollo, Ares, and Oaktree	Jun 15, 2021
3.	Amazon	Jun 15, 2021
4.	Boeing	May 26, 2021
5.	Goldman Sachs	May 21, 2021
6.	Corporate Call to Action: Co...	May 18, 2021

1 - 100 / 259   ⌄ ⌃

As of August 2021, 261 corporations have pledged $67.186 billion to BLM. Cash disbursed so far only totals $652 million. Net income for the firms making pledges equals $747.5 billion; BLM Pledges represent 8.9% of net income.

I submitted a request to the US Securities and Exchange Commission (SEC) to develop mandatory rules for public companies to disclose high-quality, comparable, decision-useful information concerning BLM Pledge fulfillment. You can view the request at www.sec.gov/rules/petitions/2021/petn4-774.pdf. You can submit comments at https://www.sec.gov/comments/4-774/4-774.htm.

I believe that it may make sense for minority firms to monitor developments in this area. I also believe it makes sense to reach out to each and every corporation and foundation that made a BLM Pledge if you are an African American seeking capital. To facilitate this activity, I have listed data showing all of the 261 organizations in the appendix.

Before you reach out, I suggest studying this issue carefully. The following are links to a series of newspaper and magazine articles on the subject. I have also included text from my request to the SEC.

In an interview with Pulitzer Prize–winning journalist Stephen Henderson titled "Some Companies Have Done Better Than Others Keeping Racial Justice Pledges" on NPR's Detroit Today dated May 28, 2021, I stated that

> Last year, after the murder of George Floyd, 251 American companies vowed to combat systemic racism within their own organizations. In aggregate, these companies pledged $65 billion to bolster their diversity and equity initiatives. One year later, only $500 million has been allocated toward these efforts.

> American companies have the resources to honor these pledges, but structural and cultural problems, as well as a lack of accountability, are hindering their ability to follow through on their promises.

https://wdet.org/posts/2021/05/28/91024-some-companies-have-done-better-than-others-keeping-racial-justice-pledges/

Black Lives Matter: Corporate America Has Pledged $1.678 Billion So Far. June 10, 2020. www.blackenterprise.com/black-lives-matter-corporate-america-has-pledged-1-678-billion-so-far/

Valuable Changemaking for Remote Washington Semester Program Interns. www.american.edu/news/20200825-washington-semester-program.cfm

Six Companies Account for 70% of Corporate Black Lives Matter Pledges. https://youtu.be/t7aqn7oGGj0

$50 Billion And A Year Later the World Still Searches for Accountability After George Floyd's Death. https://tpinsights.com/2021/05/24/50-billion-and-a-year-later-the-world-still-searches-for-accountability-after-george-floyds-death/

American companies pledged $50 billion to Black communities. Most of it hasn't materialized. https://fortune.com/2021/05/06/us-companies-black-communities-money-50-billion/

Are CEOs living up to the pledges they made after George Floyd's murder? https://creativeinvest.com/FinTimesMay2021.pdf

BLM Pledges and Developments in Corporate Governance

Recently, signal institutional and retail investors have demanded and received significant corporate governance–related changes at major energy corporations.[1] These activities show that investors are now more effectively using new information on a range of issues, many of which are focused on uncovering and understanding long-term performance and risk management factors impacting public reporting companies. Clearly, norms of business reporting activities are changing rapidly in response to new social concerns.

So it is with issues regarding African Americans and corporate performance, perhaps the most contentious of social factors impacting shareholder value. To lower the discomfort (and subsequent defensiveness) many whites experience when confronted by information about African American inequality and injustice, discussions around race are now known as "diversity-related" issues and have been expanded to include additional racial groups, like Asian and Hispanics, gender-related factors, and sexual preference/behavior-related issues.[2]

Public companies offer additional information to address diversity-related investor preferences and regulatory requirements. The Congress of the United States has recognized that adequate diversity-related data reporting standards do not exist.[3]

Many, but not all, public companies are voluntarily producing "diversity reports" to meet the requests from investors for information related to

---

[1] According to NBC News, "Exxon Mobil lost at least two board seats to an activist hedge fund and shareholders at Chevron endorsed a call to further reduce its emissions." See "Climate activists score wins against Exxon, Shell and Chevron." Online at www.nbcnews.com/business/energy/climate-activists-score-wins-against-exxon-shell-chevron-n1268705

[2] The nature of white supremacy is to use a "divide and conquer" strategy to maintain the strongest possible hold on power. The dilution of diversity efforts is a real-world example of how this is done.

[3] See H. R. 2123 – To amend the Dodd-Frank Wall Street Reform and Consumer Protection Act to require regulated entities to provide information necessary for the Offices of Minority and Women Inclusion to carry out their duties. Online at www.congress.gov/117/bills/hr2123/BILLS-117hr2123ih.pdf

company performance in these areas. Despite having laws in place[4] to support corporate reporting in this area, when it comes to Blacks, substantial issues and problems with the nature, timing, and extent of these voluntary diversity disclosures remain. Thus, there is a need to develop a comprehensive framework for clearer, more consistent, more complete, and more easily comparable information relevant to companies' long-term performance as it relates to African Americans, specifically BLM Pledge "commitments." Such a framework would better inform investors and would provide clarity to America's public companies on providing auditable information to investors.

Identifying Pledges

Capturing data on corporate donations and commitments is by far the most essential element of the process. Corporate press releases and social media postings were utilized and sourced in creating our list. These direct citations were preferred to news articles and other listings, since they legally tie a company to its commitment. The total BLM Pledge, whether an immediate donation or decade-long commitment, is listed, described, and summed.

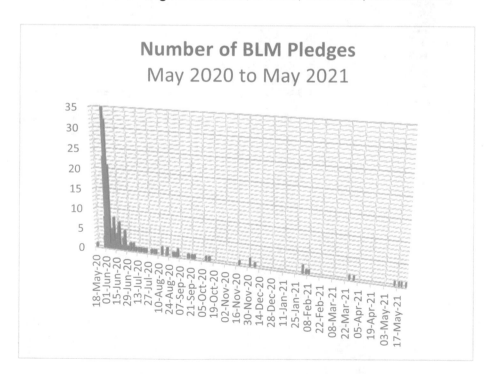

Number of BLM Pledges
May 2020 to May 2021

---

[4] Section 342(b) of the Dodd-Frank Wall Street Reform and Consumer Protection Act (12 U.S.C. 5452(b)).

Pledges in July, 2020

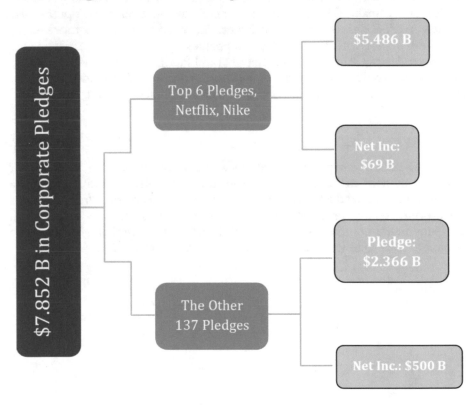

Pledges in July, 2021

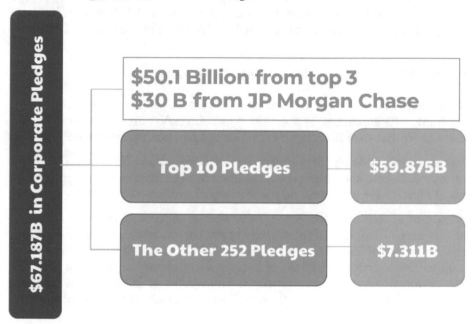

$67.187B in Corporate Pledges

$50.1 Billion from top 3
$30 B from JP Morgan Chase

Top 10 Pledges — **$59.875B**

The Other 252 Pledges — **$7.311B**

Starting in the summer of 2020 and continuing to the present, I classified corporate BLM donations by levels of trust and accountability. This allowed a defensible estimate of how much BLM Pledge money has been reliably spent and utilized.

BLM Pledges and Global Competitiveness

The lack of performance with respect to BLM Pledges will impair the competitiveness of US capital markets and America's public companies by showing that they are untrustworthy. Thus, requiring additional BLM Pledge disclosure will enhance competitiveness.

BLM Pledge Disclosure and the Free Rider Problem

Enforcing standardized reporting requirements will also serve to reduce or eliminate the "free rider" problem. Public firms making significant BLM Pledges typically spend a great deal of effort, time, and money to develop meaningful pledges. We have observed, however, a number of organizations that have made inauthentic BLM promises but received the same positive regard granted to other, more serious and significant BLM Pledge efforts. This "positive regard" increases long-term shareholder value. A consistent BLM Pledge reporting taxonomy will allow for the analysis of BLM "commitments" and pledges and, hopefully, help reveal which pledges are sincere and which are not.

BLM Pledges and White Supremacy

White supremacy and racism impose massive costs on the market and on the economy.[5] Paradoxically, in the two group Black/White cases, most of the damage from racism is imposed on white people, not Black people.

Some white people's preference for discrimination contributes to this outcome. People and institutions discriminate because they have a preference (taste) for it.[6] They understand there is a cost and are willing to pay it.

For example, consider the economic crisis[7] of 2006 to 2016, which resulted in the loss of millions of jobs, cost thousands of lives, and imposed $19.2 trillion[8] in actual losses, according to the US Department of the Treasury. It led[9] to the election, in 2016, of a true demagogue as president and the imposition of additional[10] social costs. The 2008 and 2020 downturns were entirely predictable[11] and preventable. They were facilitated by racially biased,

---

[5] See www.impactinvesting.online/2019/03/the-economic-and-social-cost-of-racism.html

[6] Gary S. Becker (1957, 1971, 2nd ed.). The Economics of Discrimination. Chicago, University of Chicago Press.

[7] Global Market Turmoil Graphic and Financial Crisis Calendar Graphic, Creative Investment Research, November, 2009.

[8] Financial Crisis Response in Charts. US Dept. of Treasury. April 13 2012. Online at www.treasury.gov/resource-center/data-chart-center/Documents/20120413_FinancialCrisisResponse.pdf

[9] "Why Trump Will Win." June 11, 2016. www.linkedin.com/pulse/why-trump-win-william-michael-cunningham-am-mba

[10] U.S. COVID deaths as of May 30, 2021: 594,300. https://coronavirus.jhu.edu/us-map

[11] See Supreme Court of the United States. No. 97–5066. William Michael Cunningham, Petitioner v. Board of Governors of the Federal Reserve System. Petition for writ of certiorari to the United States Court of Appeals for the District of Columbia Circuit. United States Court of Appeals FOR THE DISTRICT OF COLUMBIA CIRCUIT. No. 97-1256 William Michael Cunningham, APPELLANT v. Board of Governors of the Federal Reserve System, Appellee. Decided April 30, 1997. United States Court of Appeals FOR THE DISTRICT OF COLUMBIA CIRCUIT. No. 98-1459 William Michael Cunningham, APPELLANT v. Board of Governors of the Federal Reserve System, Appellee. October, 1998. Also, see: This Week in Socially Responsible Investing, October 3, 2011. (Published October 2, 2011) http://eepurl.com/gage9

incompetent[12] product development and distribution strategy that ensured the public, starting with Black people but moving rapidly to whites, would be damaged. Financial marketplace institutions did so, in part, because they were allowed to do so by federal regulators captured by the financial services industry[13] and incapable of competently protecting the public interest.

Further costs are imposed on racist whites by their need to continually monitor the relative economic positions of various racial groups and to act out based on the information revealed. The January 6, 2021, insurrection at the US Capitol is but one example of this.

Other costs include the need to lie and expenditures related to covering up various illegal behaviors.

The petitioner believes disclosure will, over time, reduce the cost of racism and discrimination.

BLM Pledges and the Lack of Ethics in the Marketplace

A growing lack of ethics in the marketplace means relying on voluntary disclosures is unwise and likely inefficient. We have described several cases where public company corporate management unfairly transferred value from outsider to insider shareholders.[14] These abuses have been linked to an abandonment of ethical principles.

Faulty market practices mask a company's true value and misallocate capital by moving investment dollars from deserving companies to unworthy companies. (BLM Pledges are made with the hope of enhancing a company's value. False statements hide true value.) Market institutions cannot survive continuously elevated levels of fraud.

---

[12] Document 45, filed 09/24/2013. Opinion and Order, US v. Wells Fargo. 12 Civ, 7527 (JMF).

[13] George Stigler, "The Theory of Economic Regulation," Bell Journal of Economics, 2, 1971: 3–21.

[14] See Comment Letter (sec.gov) and see Amicus Brief filed by William Michael Cunningham in City of Oakland v. Wells Fargo. Court of Appeals for the Ninth Circuit. Case number 19-15169. https://creativeinvest.com/WellFargoNinthCir.pdf

BLM Pledge List

The following is our list of organizations making BLM Pledges. The data was compiled by Andrew Taber, Impact Investing Analyst, Creative Investment Research.

Name of Corporation	Date of Pledge	Starting Fund/Amount Donated
#Merky and CEO Stormzy	6/11/2020	$ 12,485,350
Adidas	6/10/2020	$ 120,000,000
AIG	6/1/2020	$ 500,000
Airbnb	6/1/2020	$ 500,000
Allbirds	5/30/2020	$ -
Altria	6/5/2020	$ 5,000,000
Amazon	6/3/2020	$ 10,000,000
Amazon	6/15/2021	$ 150,000,000
Ameriprise	6/5/2020	$ 150,000
Anastasia Beverly Hills	6/1/2020	$ 1,000,000
Andreesen Horowitz	6/3/2020	$ 2,200,000
Apollo, Ares, and Oaktree	6/15/2021	$ 90,000,000
Apple	6/11/2020	$ 100,000,000
Applied Materials	6/1/2020	$ 100,000
Aritzia	5/31/2020	$ 100,000
Articulate	6/1/2020	$ 100,000
AT&T	7/30/2020	$ 10,000,000
Autodesk	6/4/2020	$ 75,000
Bad Robot Productions	6/1/2020	$ 10,000,000
Bank of America	6/2/2020	$ 1,000,000,000

Bank of America with Smithsonian	6/8/2020	$	25,000,000
Baxter	2/8/2021	$	2,000,000
BBC	6/22/2020	$	117,518,000
Ben & Jerry's (Owned by Unilever)	5/18/2020	$	-
Billie (owned by P&G)	5/31/2020	$	100,000
Biogen	9/3/2020	$	10,000,000
Biossance (Owned by Amyris)	5/31/2020	$	100,000
Bloomberg Philanthropies	8/20/2020	$	100,000,000
Blue Cross MA	2/1/2021	$	350,000
Boeing	8/28/2020	$	10,600,000
Boeing	5/26/2021	$	500,000
Bombas	6/3/2020	$	250,000
Boy Smells	5/31/2020	$	10,000
Brooklinen	5/31/2020	$	-
Brooks Running (Owned by Berkshire Hathaway)	6/3/2020	$	250,000
BTS and Big Hit Entertainment	6/14/2020	$	1,000,000
Bumble	6/10/2020	$	1,000,000
California Endowment	6/23/2020	$	225,000,000
Capital Group	6/10/2020	$	2,000,000
Capital One	6/4/2020	$	10,000,000
CBRE	6/9/2020	$	2,000,000
Central San Diego Black Chamber of Commerce	6/10/2020	$	1,000,000

CEO Box	5/29/2020	$	500,000
CEO Dropbox	6/3/2020	$	500,000
CEO Twitter	6/3/2020	$	3,000,000
Charter Commnications	6/11/2020	$	10,000,000
Chipotle	6/5/2020	$	1,000,000
Cisco	6/1/2020	$	5,000,000
Cisco	9/23/2020	$	100,000,000
CitiGroup	6/28/2020	$	1,000,000,000
Citizens Bank (Financial Group)	6/25/2020	$	750,000
Clif Bar	6/1/2020	$	100,000
CoBank	6/17/2020	$	500,000
Coca-Cola	6/3/2020	$	2,500,000
Cocokind	6/1/2020	$	10,000
Coinbase	6/4/2020	$	250,000
ColourPop	5/29/2020	$	300,000
Comcast Corp	6/8/2020	$	100,000,000
Comerica Bank	6/19/2020	$	1,000,000
Comerica Bank	8/19/2020	$	10,000,000
Constellation	6/29/2020	$	100,000,000
Corporate Call to Action: Coalition for Equity and Opportunity	5/18/2021	$	10,000,000,000
Costco	8/31/2020	$	25,000,000
Cox Enterprises	6/5/2020	$	1,000,000
Deciem	5/31/2020	$	100,000
Delta Dental of CA	6/3/2020	$	100,000

Diplomacy Worldwide	6/3/2020	$	-
Discover	7/6/2020	$	5,000,000
Disney	6/3/2020	$	5,000,000
Disney	3/30/2021	$	1,000,000
DocuSign	6/3/2020	$	500,000
DocuSign	6/3/2020	$	500,000
Doordash	6/3/2020	$	1,000,000
Doris Duke Charitable Foundation, Ford Foundation, W.K. Kellogg Foundation, the John D. & Catherine T. MacArthur Foundation, and the Andrew W. Mellon Foundation	6/11/2020	$	1,700,000,000
Dow Chemical	11/18/2020	$	5,100,000
E TRADE	6/15/2020	$	1,250,000
E.l.f Beauty	5/31/2020	$	25,000
Eaze	5/31/2020	$	25,000
Edelman	6/18/2020	$	1,000,000
Electronic Arts	6/2/2020	$	1,000,000
Emmy's Organics	6/1/2020	$	-
Etsy	6/1/2020	$	1,000,000
Everlane	6/3/2020	$	150,000
Evo	6/1/2020	$	15,000
EY	6/11/2020	$	7,000,000
Fabletics	5/30/2020	$	50,000
Facebook	6/1/2020	$	10,000,000
Facebook	6/18/2020	$	200,000,000

Farmacy	5/30/2020	$	10,000
Farmers Insurance	6/3/2020	$	250,000
Fashion Nova	6/3/2020	$	1,000,000
Fedex	6/21/2020	$	500,000
Fifth Third Bank	9/16/2020	$	1,200,000
Fifth Third Bank	12/7/2020	$	2,800,000,000
Fila	5/31/2020	$	100,000
Flamingo and Harry's (Edgewell)	6/1/2020	$	500,000
Foot Locker	4/27/2021	$	200,000,000
Ganni (Owned by LVMH)	6/1/2020	$	100,000
Gap Inc.	5/31/2020	$	250,000
Glossier	5/30/2020	$	1,000,000
Glow Recipe	5/30/2020	$	10,000
GM	6/5/2020	$	10,000,000
GoFundMe	5/31/2020	$	500,000
Goldman Sachs	6/3/2020	$	10,000,000
Goldman Sachs	5/21/2021	$	10,100,000,000
Google	6/3/2020	$	25,000,000
Google	6/3/2020	$	2,500,000
Google	6/17/2020	$	175,000,000
Google	6/17/2021	$	50,000,000
Google (Alphabet)	6/3/2020	$	12,000,000
Grameen America	5/13/2021	$	1,300,000,000
GrubHub	6/3/2020	$	1,000,000
Guru	6/4/2020	$	30,000
H&M	6/1/2020	$	500,000

H-E-B	6/2/2020	$	1,000,000
Herbivore	5/30/2020	$	-
Hinterland Games	6/1/2020	$	10,000
Holland & Knight LLP	9/3/2020	$	100,000
Home Depot	6/1/2020	$	1,000,000
Honest Beauty	5/31/2020	$	100,000
Honeywell	6/17/2020	$	2,000,000
HourGlass Cosmetics	6/1/2020	$	100,000
HP	6/24/2020	$	500,000
HumbleBundle (Owned by J2 Global)	6/2/2020	$	1,000,000
ILIA	6/1/2020	$	50,000
Intel	5/31/2020	$	1,000,000
JP Morgan Chase	10/8/2020	$	30,000,000,000
Juvia's Place	8/13/2020	$	300,000
Kaiser Permanente (with LISC)	6/25/2020	$	100,000,000
Kirkland & Ellis	6/5/2020	$	5,000,000
Kohl's	8/20/2020	$	1,000,000
Kosas	5/31/2020	$	20,000
KPMG	6/5/2020	$	500,000
Kroger	6/5/2020	$	5,000,000
Kroger	2/1/2021	$	-
Lam Research	6/2/2020	$	1,000,000
Lego	6/3/2020	$	4,000,000
Levi's	5/31/2020	$	200,000
Liberty Mutual	6/6/2020	$	1,000,000

Liberty Mutual	7/15/2020	$	1,000,000
LISC	11/19/2020	$	925,000,000
Love Wellness	6/3/2020	$	25,000
Lowe's (with LISC)	7/16/2020	$	5,000,000
Lululemon	5/29/2020	$	250,000
Lyft	6/1/2020	$	500,000
Manulife Financial	6/25/2020	$	3,500,000
Mastercard	9/17/2020	$	500,000,000
McDonald's	5/30/2020	$	1,000,000
MetLife	6/18/2020	$	5,000,000
Microsoft	6/5/2020	$	1,500,000
Microsoft	6/23/2020	$	150,000,000
MLB	6/10/2020	$	1,000,000
MLB + MLBPA	9/21/2020	$	10,000,000
Morgan Stanley	6/9/2020	$	5,000,000
Morgan Stanley	6/11/2020	$	10,000,000
Morton Salt	7/23/2020	$	600,000
National Football League	6/11/2020	$	250,000,000
Nationwide	6/12/2020	$	1,000,000
NBA	8/5/2020	$	300,000,000
Necessaire	5/31/2020	$	10,000
Netflix	6/15/2020	$	5,000,000
Netflix (with LISC)	6/30/2020	$	100,000,000
Netflix CEO	6/2/2020	$	1,000,000
Netflix CEO	6/17/2020	$	120,000,000
Neutrogena (Owned by Johnson & Johnson)	6/1/2020	$	200,000

Niantic	6/3/2020	$	5,150,000
Nike	6/5/2020	$	40,000,000
Nike (Michael Jordan and Jordan Brand)	6/5/2020	$	100,000,000
Obsidian Entertainment (owned by Xbox owned by Microsoft)	6/4/2020	$	25,000
Old National Bank	7/20/2020	$	50,000
Old National Bank	2/5/2021	$	75,000
Open Society Foundations	7/13/2020	$	220,000,000
PagerDuty	6/9/2020	$	500,000
Patagonia	5/31/2020	$	100,000
Patreon	6/3/2020	$	50,000
Paula's Choice	6/1/2020	$	10,000
Paypal	6/11/2020	$	535,000,000
Peloton	5/31/2020	$	500,000
Peloton	6/23/2020	$	100,000,000
PepsiCo	6/16/2020	$	445,000,000
Pillsbury Winthrop Shaw Pittman	6/15/2020	$	11,000,000
Pinterest	6/2/2020	$	1,500,000
PNC	6/18/2020	$	1,050,000,000
Pokemon Company	6/3/2020	$	200,000
Poshmark	6/3/2020	$	100,000
Procter & Gamble	6/3/2020	$	5,000,000
PSEG	6/18/2020	$	1,000,000
PSEG	3/25/2021	$	1,000,000
Purple Carrot	6/1/2020	$	40,000

PwC	6/4/2020	$	1,000,000
QVC	6/18/2020	$	1,000,000
Raytheon Technologies	12/1/2020	$	25,000,000
Resource Generation	6/17/2020	$	5,000,000
Riot Games	6/5/2020	$	1,000,000
Riot Games (owned by Tencent)	6/5/2020	$	10,000,000
RobinHood	6/10/2020	$	500,000
Royal Bank of Canada	6/5/2020	$	1,500,000
Royal Bank of Canada	7/6/2020	$	150,000,000
Rubio Butterfield Memorial Foundation: CEO Slack, CEO Away	5/31/2020	$	1,000,000
S&P Global	6/4/2020	$	1,000,000
Sallie Mae Fund	6/25/2020	$	4,250,000
Santander Bank	7/2/2020	$	5,200,000
Sephora (Owned by LVMH)	5/30/2020	$	1,000,000
Sequoia Capital	6/1/2020	$	-
ServiceTitan	6/5/2020	$	100,000
SheaMoisture	6/5/2020	$	100,000
Shopify	6/1/2020	$	1,000,000
Siebert Williams Shank (with Microsoft)	8/13/2020	$	250,000,000
SoFi	6/1/2020	$	1,000,000
SoftBank Group Corp	6/3/2020	$	100,000,000
Sony Interactive Entertainment	6/1/2020	$	-

Sony Music Group (Sony as whole)	6/5/2020	$	100,000,000
Southern Company	12/1/2020	$	200,000,000
Southwest Airlines	6/16/2020	$	500,000
Spanx	5/31/2020	$	200,000
Spotify	6/3/2020	$	11,000,000
Square	9/24/2020	$	100,000,000
Square Enix	6/2/2020	$	250,000
SquareSpace	6/15/2020	$	500,000
Starbucks	6/4/2020	$	1,000,000
Starbucks	1/12/2021	$	100,000,000
Stripe	7/2/2020	$	500,000
Subaru	6/17/2020	$	500,000
Sunday Riley	5/31/2020	$	50,000
Supercell	6/2/2020	$	-
T. Rowe Price	6/18/2020	$	2,000,000
Target	6/5/2020	$	10,000,000
TD Ameritrade	7/21/2020	$	500,000
TELUS	6/3/2020	$	50,000
Texas Instruments	8/3/2020	$	1,000,000
Thatgamecompany	6/2/2020	$	20,000
The Body Shop	6/2/2020	$	10,000
The Wing	6/1/2020	$	200,000
TikTok	6/1/2020	$	4,000,000
TJX (TJ Maxx)	6/10/2020	$	10,000,000
Toms	6/1/2020	$	100,000
Travelers	6/8/2020	$	1,000,000

U.S. Bank	6/5/2020	$	116,000,000
Uber	5/31/2020	$	1,000,000
Ubisoft	6/2/2020	$	100,000
UGG/Deckers	6/3/2020	$	500,000
UnitedHealth Group	6/1/2020	$	5,000,000
UnitedHealth Group	6/1/2020	$	10,000,000
Universal Music Group	6/4/2020	$	25,000,000
UPS	6/8/2020	$	4,200,000
USAA	10/12/2020	$	50,000,000
Vanguard	6/26/2020	$	100,000
Vaquera	5/31/2020	$	-
Verizon	6/1/2020	$	10,000,000
Viacom CBS Networks	6/5/2020	$	5,000,000
Walmart	6/5/2020	$	100,000,000
Warby Parker (Owned by EssilorLuxottica)	6/1/2020	$	1,000,000
Warner Music Group	6/3/2020	$	100,000,000
Webster	6/15/2020	$	100,000
Wells Fargo	7/9/2020	$	400,000,000
Wendy's	6/3/2020	$	500,000
WeWork	6/1/2020	$	2,000,000
Whoop	6/8/2020	$	20,000
Yelp	6/4/2020	$	500,000
Youtube (Owned by Google)	6/12/2020	$	101,000,000
Yum! Brands	6/25/2020	$	100,000,000

We also have a list of organizations receiving support from corporations making BLM Pledges. I suggest you reach out to both the corporations and to the organizations on the receiving end. (You will have to google the entities to get contact information.)

For more, see `https://blacklivesmattercorporatepledges.com/`.

I

Index

A

Asian Chambers of Commerce, 118

B

Banks, 135
    documentation, 137
    dollar amount, 135
    employment, 137
    income, 136
    loans, 136
    loan security, 137
    maturity, 135
    time period, 136
Bitcoin, 108, 128, 155
Black and brown entrepreneurs, 146
Black Chambers of Commerce, 117
Black community, 113, 154, 159
Black Lives Matter (BLM) movement, 2, 147, 157
Black people, 152
    collaborative/cooperative effort, 154
    focus on human needs, 154
    normal, 154
BLM Pledge commitments, 163, 181
    competitiveness, 165
    disclosure, 165
    marketplace, 167
    white supremacy, 166, 167
Business credit, 132, 135, 137

Business lending resources
    Fundbox, 133
    Kabbage, 134
    LoanBuilder, 133
    OnDeck, 134
    summary, 134
Business Loan program, 130
Business ownership, 146

C

Capitalism, 151
Cash App, 130
Certification, 47, 99
Chamber of Commerce, 112
    counts, 115
    discounts/benefits, 114
    join, 114
Community Development Block Grant (CDBG), 104
Community Development Financial Institutions (CDFI), 104
Compass Group, 123
Corporate donations, 163
Corporate governance, 162
Corporate supplier diversity programs, 120
COVID-19, 2, 43, 105, 146
Creative Investment
    Research, 159, 169, 181

© William Michael Cunningham 2021
W. M. Cunningham, *Thriving As a Minority-Owned Business in Corporate America*,
https://doi.org/10.1007/978-1-4842-7240-4

Printed in the United States
by Baker & Taylor Publisher Services